BOOKS OF POETRY BY

Robert Hillyer

Collected Poems

Collected
Poems

ROBERT HILLYER

1961

ALFRED A. KNOPF · NEW YORK

L. C. catalog card number: 61–8531

THIS IS A BORZOI BOOK,

PUBLISHED BY ALFRED A. KNOPF, INC.

Manufactured in the United States of America.
Published simultaneously in Canada
by McClelland & Stewart, Ltd.

FIRST EDITION

To MY WIFE JEANNE;
  MY SON AND HIS FAMILY,
    STANLEY AND LAURA,
      ELIZABETH AND FRANCESCA

Acknowledgments

Some twenty-five of the poems in this volume originally appeared in *The New Yorker,* and twenty (including the section called "Letters") in *The Atlantic Monthly.* Many were published in distinguished periodicals that no longer exist, and whose names are part of the history of our literature, such as *The Smart Set, The Dial, The Hound and Horn, The Seven Arts, The Outlook, The Forum, The American Caravan, The Freeman,* and *The New Adelphi* (London). Various others have appeared in *The American Scholar, Harper's Magazine, L. A., The Literary Review, The Lyric, The New Republic, Poetry: A Magazine of Verse, The New York Times Book Review,* and *The Poetry Dial.* I make grateful acknowledgment to the editors of all these publications, past and present, for permission, where necessary, to reprint and for many pleasant associations through the years.

Contents

VARIATIONS ON A THEME, SONNETS, PASTORALS, PROTHALAMION

LYRICS
AND SHORTER POEMS · I ·

Manorbier

It is green with ivy
But the stones are crisscrossed
With cracks and crannies,
Tooth marks of the frost.
The roofless tower,
The sundered wall,
The gaping lancet—
Frost gnaws them all.
Time in transit
Measured by years
Has emptied the hall,
Rusted the spears.
The long rains fall
Where the marriage bed
Saw the virgin a wife
And the mother dead,
Saw the birth of the son
And the warrior head
White on the pillow
Stained with red.

Now it is summer,
The swans float
Each with its double
On the scummy moat.
If you hear the fiddler
Playing his fiddle
It's the wind in the crannies
With dust in its throat.
If you hear the drummer
Tapping his drum

It's a dead branch hanging
Swinging and banging,
Summoning no one—
There is no one to come.

I was born in a chamber
Under the eaves;
The room I remember
And the sound of leaves
And the sound of ocean
And of ships come home
When we ran with our welcome
Kneedeep through the foam.
With toy sword brandished
And toy horn blowing,
Child cries to the father,
"The old raven is dead!"
And the father to the child:
"Your mother is dead!"
And somebody said,
"He speaks of the raven
When his mother is dead."

In the garden by moonlight
Each leaf on the rose bush
A silver flake,
A ghost of a flame!
Hearing voices, the loveless one
Fired by their passion
Fled down to the lake
Where a tall lady came.

"Tomorrow at sunset,"
She said to her lover,
"Look up to my window

And I will be there."
She glimmered away,
And faint like a halo
The moon on her hair.

Most beautiful lady,
How slowly the snail
Through the gray dust lengthens
His rainbow trail.
On the steps of the sunset
Did I find you—or not?
How should you remember
When your lover forgot?

Is there nobody now
Who can speak with my speech
But the wind in the ruin,
The waves on the beach?
There are hundreds of cities
Out there beyond reach,
Three thousand miles over
The sea whence I came.
I built them myself;
I left this to the weather,
And forgot my own name.
I will go up the stairway
That ends in the air,
I will stand in the chapel
And offer a prayer
To saints who for ages
Have not been there.
I will lean out of windows
That have no top
And look far below me
A dizzy drop

To the moat and the cliff
And beyond to the beach
And beyond to the ocean,
Where the eyes stop.

Why did I leave
   this house like a Viking?
Why did I leave it
   for frosts to crack?
Did the stairway lead me
   then to disaster?
Did the door ajar
   show the flame and the rack?
I have forgotten the cause of my going—
And even the cause of my coming back.

Some things with me
   are the never-dying,
All of us cursëd
   with time's effacement:
The ivy vine grown
   so black has forgotten
The beginning tendril
   that clung to the basement;
The gap in the wall has forgotten the window—
And I, the face that looked down from the casement.

Now is the season when the whole world over
The herds are munching the ripe clover;
The green baby-hair of the crops to come
Is ruffled by the wind; the may-flies hum
In the air, and the bees intermittently humming
Dive to one flower and drone to a sweeter:
This is the mating-song season, at evening
When the lover listens his love will be coming.

But summer like winter
Conspiring slowly
To throw down the mighty
And exalt the lowly
Is gnawing at walls
All but time held holy.
By tendrils of ivy
The stones are split;
Trees shoulder the ingles
Where earls would sit,
And the ants drag the mortar
Away, bit by bit.

Who is my brother?
Who is my friend?
The song does not falter
Though the singer end.
But I, the last singer,
Forgetting my song
One summer morning
A thousand years long,
Have gone up the stairway
That ends in the air,
Surprising dead saints
With the ghost of a prayer,
And looked out of windows
That have no top,
To the beach, to the ocean,
Where the eyes stop.
But the mind will not stop.
The heart will not stop.

The Scar

FOR forty years and more my hand has shown
The scar where once a fishhook tore the flesh.
The body bears these grudges of its own.
The mind would let them go, but scars refresh
Unwilling memory. Owing to this mark,
One summer moment at Menemsha Bight
Stays with me like a date cut in the bark
Of some old tree, though not another sight
Remains from that day, nor would any thought,
Except for this indelible reminder.
Each seven years a bodily change is wrought,
Yet cells renew the scar. The heart is kinder
That wears its wounds invisibly until
All names are lost, lacking a cicatrice.
The hand recalls the embedded fishhook still,
When love and memory long have been at peace.

Overture

THIS record played in the room has lost all the music
I heard that night far out at sea:
I was alone in my sailboat, the sail breathing
slackly the light airs, the ripple at the bow
a placid murmur, and the tall mast
a slim black needle plying the North Star—
no one within miles of me, except where to starboard
the lights of a tug signalled three barges in tow,
and beyond that, off the invisible shoreline,
the flashing white and red of the lighthouse—
this music came from my radio in the darkness
and told me that I must sail alone
until, in some harbor known to the composer

but which I could barely surmise,
I arrived at dawn and dropped anchor and rowed
   ashore
in another dream beyond the starlight of this one,
the friends I have never found crowding the wharf,
waiting with welcome. The music came to an end,
but the eternal ship moved on to a rhythm
deeper than the keel or the waters under the keel,
and higher than the North Star over the masthead
   riding.

April Morning

THE day is as frail
As gossamer.
The light is pale.
The April stir
Of wind and wings
Is soft as fur.
The water sings
In silver hush
From hillside springs
To lakeside rush.
Today is waking
The robin, the thrush,
The first note shaking
The gray suspense,
The first love-making
Of innocence . . .
The day so frail,
The light so pale.

The Muffled Gong

I DO not hit the gong quite squarely
Lest my full feeling should be known.
A glancing blow is best—Oh, rarely
More than a murmurous undertone.

Here on this terrace, pine-surrounded,
Where mountains darken echoing lakes,
I've learned how gently must be sounded
Tones that the faintest touch awakes.

See, now I strike—you scarcely hear it;
Muted and true the sound. It rings
In the inner ear; it is the spirit
Of lost and unsubstantial things:

Love, for example, and the lover,
Who now can be evoked no more,
Or dawns we never can recover
In landscapes we are homesick for,

Which now, as in the past, would cloy us
Could we renew them for a day.
Time and its years do not destroy us,
But learning that it was not they.

There! Once again a light vibration.
You hear the undertone of course?
Perhaps some other incarnation
Will find me striking it full force.

But even now I shun this notion
Behind the enigmatic years—
Such clang and clangor of emotion!
Such thawing of unseemly tears!

Julia's Room

HE WENT up the dark stairs and knocked at Julia's
    door;
It opened, and a blade of light cut the dim hall,
But the girl was a stranger, and when he spoke to her
She could not—or would not—understand at all.
She looked at him a moment—horrified, he thought—
Then slammed the door shut.

Bewildered, he guessed that while he was away
Julia must have invited a friend he had never known;
Sometimes when she asked an old friend to stay
She moved to the attic room and gave up her own.
So he climbed the second flight, but that floor was dark
As rain-drenched bark.

"Julia!" he called, but no light flashed on.
"Julia!" he called down the stair-well gloom.
. . . "Whoever you are, for God's sake be gone!"
The strange woman cried from Julia's own room.
Then he remembered it was fifty years ago,
And he melted like snow.

Reflections in Still Water

I WATCHED the pond without lifting my eyes;
Shadow of leaves on shadow skies;
Scarves of colour twining through haze
And a bright bird flying with wings ablaze;
A bird flying over, the day in flight,
And I watched him pass without lifting my eyes.
It was enough, the shadow of delight,
The shadow of a bird over shadow skies.

The first white star unbound her hair;
The water trembled and she was there
Setting her foot on the darkening mirror
While round her the trees of night leaned nearer;
They gathering dark, she gathering light,
And I watched the pond without lifting my eyes.
It was enough, the shadow of night,
The shadow of a star in the shadow skies.

Doctor Samuel Johnson

DOCTOR Samuel Johnson
Is riding to hounds,
His bulk is ungainly,
His posture astounds.
His wig is awry
And his breathing is short,
But the Doctor would die
Before leaving the sport.

Doctor Johnson at sixty
Is voyaging forth
On a small, leaky vessel
To visit the North.
In the far Hebrides
When the youngsters grow pale
At the fling of the seas,
He advises more sail.

Doctor Johnson's a bully,
A sophist, a clown;
He is meek with the boobies
And roars the wise down.
He is also the bravest,

The most honest man,
The gayest when gravest,
The best of our clan.

Doctor Samuel Johnson
Would take great offence
That I speak of him present
So long vanished hence.
By niceness impassioned,
His mood, like his tense,
Was fantasy fashioned
From strict common sense.

Song

VERSE is a turning
Around and around,
A gold autumn leaf
Turning on air
From a poem to spring
And summer gone by,
A hovering accent,
A late butterfly,
Till it touches the ground
And perishes there
As song into silence
Following sound,
But with never a reason
For memory's yearning,
No reason for grief,
For so falls the leaf,
And so falls the season,
Turning, returning.

The Seagoing Farmer

Robert Hillyer

CANDIDA said to me, "Where are you going tomorrow?"
"I am going to sea," I said, "to a livelier land.
The plow is rusting away in the half-tilled furrow;
This country has grown too tame for my mariner's hand."
The wind sang like the wind through a schooner's shrouds,
And the hills billowed with shadows from billowing clouds.

Candida said to me, "So you will leave me. I thought so.
You and your islands where everything's set for a feast!
But vows and faith mean something, at least I was taught so,
Besides, there is nothing but war in your fabulous East."
"So much the better," I answered, "I'd rather be dust
In the storm of the world than a creature of habit and rust."

Candida looked at me smiling. I shifted and mumbled,
"Well, you can smile, for I know you have heard this
          before."
She turned on her heel and left me, she knew I was
          humbled.
I shouted, "O can't a man dream in spite of the War?"
The sun was the golden disk of a Viking shield
As I laughed and went back to the plow and finished the
          field.

The Assassination

"Do YOU not find something very strange about
          him?"
Asked the First Fate.
"Very strange indeed," answered the Second Fate,
"He is immune to change."
"Yes, he is always young," complained the First Fate.

"He never heeds us," said the Second,
"I, for example, have often called and beckoned."
"We must kill him while he sleeps."
"He does not sleep."
"Then we must make him weep."
"He does not weep."
"Or laugh?"
"Only at his own epitaph,—
Half tears and laughter half."
"Then how to death, that worst fate,
To doom him?" said the First Fate.
"Oh, he's a clever one, as we've long reckoned,"
Answered the Second.
"But we can cope
With such a fellow, can we not,
What?"
"Could we not, say with a falling girder,
Carelessly cause an unintended murder?"
"Why not?"
"He's dead. Who said we could not cope
With this young fool. What was his name?"
"His name?"
"Of course that's not within our scope,
But just the same . . ."
"Hope was his name."
"How funny, Hope."

The Eternal Return

ALONG how many Main Streets have I walked,
Greeting my friends, commenting on the weather,
Carrying bundles, wondering as I talked
If the brown paper bags would hold together.

At Christmas time with white breath blowing thin,
In spring when garden tidings are exchanged,
In autumn with the darkness closing in
And all the winter's work to be arranged.

Wherever I have lived—and many places
Have briefly seemed my permanent abode—
The shops on Main Street and the passing faces,
Beyond all history and change of mode,

Remain the same. And if while on a walk
I should encounter people who belong
In Main Streets of my past, I'd stop to talk
Without suspecting anything was wrong.

Even if I met someone who was dead,
I would discount the fact as in a dream.
Here things that lie behind are still ahead,
And calendars less final than they seem.

External accidents of time and space
Become, on Main Street, but illusory errors,
As all my incarnations, face to face,
Repeat themselves like people in two mirrors.

I greet acquaintances unchanged as I,
Stop for a moment, comment on the weather,
And at the corner, as I say goodbye,
Pray God my paper bundles hold together.

An Old-Fashioned Fourth

THE glorious Fourth is tamed and has become
A holiday of regulated joys,
With speeches, songs, and dank officialdom,
While fireworks are proscribed as lethal toys
And nowhere seen but in the public parks
For the remote applause of girls and boys
Removed from jeopardy of flying sparks—
Spectators who are suitably astonished
When rockets bloom from coruscating arcs.
Firecrackers and brass cannon have been banished;
Torpedoes, packed in little bags of sand,
Have, with the horses they once frightened,
        vanished;
In fact, a pale decorum shrouds the land.

Once it was shrouded in gunpowder smoke
And hollow booms as giant crackers burst,
Breaking the hush as soon as daylight broke,
Continuing till nightfall, when the first
Rocket soared upward, trailing a thin blaze,
Followed by hundreds that in turn dispersed
Their Queen Anne's lace of jewel-tipped bouquets
Spearing the clouds. Meanwhile, our nether world
Glowed with the flares in green-and-scarlet haze,
And Chinese lanterns glimmered, pinwheels swirled
Their hissing firedance on the sidewalk tree—
And ah! the set piece of our flag unfurled
With forty-six stars in its galaxy!

The day dragged slowly, but at last it ended
As boys returned like battle-smudged dragoons;
A little breeze arose, the dew descended,
Then, lovelier than all, beneath the moon's

Disdainful chill, alive with warmth and light,
Floated the argosies of fire balloons
Along the driftways of the upper night.
Weaving through warps of noise their silent woofs,
They gradually cooled and sank from sight
To kindle haymows or dry shingle roofs,
Startling the darkness with tumultuous pyres
While horse-drawn engines, loud with clashing hoofs
And clanging gongs, plunged toward the scattered
        fires.

For days thereafter street and lawn were littered
With wagonloads of colorful debris;
Children were bandaged, parents were embittered,
Charred patches were revealed on grass and tree.
But, doubtless, every young incendiary
Would most enthusiastically agree
That even Christmases were secondary
To these wild holocausts that thrilled us yearly.
Concerning this, opinions well may vary;
I will but say I loved the old Fourth dearly
That threatened my survival each July;
But now it fades, and I remember merely
One bright balloon adrift in evening sky.

Miss Helen Lang

WHO now remembers Miss Helen Lang,
The piano teacher who loved to bang
Beethoven loud on the listening air
When windows were open everywhere?

In the hot suburban afternoon
Both leaves and people hung in a swoon,

Limp from the tree or limp in the swing,
Except for Miss Helen Lang, poor thing.

"Her piano keys are the keys to Hell!"
My mother said. "She plays very well,"
Answered Aunt Ella to be perverse;
Aunt Marion's "Lawsy!" was like a curse.

My aunts are dead and so is my mother;
I suppose that I and my sisters and brother
Alone remember Miss Helen Lang,
Who loved Beethoven played with a bang.

Three Songs from Ancient Egypt

I

REMEMBER me as one
Who loved your temples more than any priest,
O Watchers on the City of the Sun!
Yea, from the moment when the bark
Of the young Horus cast off from the East
Until it reached the port
Beneath the Mountain of the Dark,
My heart was on its altar in your Court.
O Mighty Ones whose faces are as bright
As lapis lazuli,
Remember me
Whose days were all too short.

II

It is pleasant to make thy mooring
Where the river spreads and darkens
Under the shadowed cedars
In the land that loveth silence.

Fair is the wind that bears thee
Over the murmur of waters,
Calm is the pool for mooring
Where the wind shall blow no longer.

There without day or morrow,
Freed from thy hate and terror,
Thou shalt be loved of silence,
And the West shall call thee Brother.

III

The fields are fat with barley and rye,
Green over green beneath blue sky;
The *bennu* bird would fly
Three days to where the sand begins.
But the granaries of my Prince are empty,
The roofs have fallen into the bins.

Beyond the fields—what then?
The Red Desert shines
Hot in the pale blue afternoon.
Here were the quarries and the mines,
And a deep well for our thirsty men.
But over the blinding waste is strewn
Silver never wrought by the smith,
And hugely full-length on the sand
One granite monolith,
Left in the place where it was hewn,
Has forgotten the temple that we planned.

The granaries of my Prince are empty,
In the House of Grain the wind is stored,
In the halls of my Prince the winds are walking,

Alas! O my Beloved, my Lord,
Is there nobody now who remembers the
   language of Egypt?

In My Library, Late Afternoon

In the dim library, my younger self
Drifts with possessive hands from shelf to shelf;
Haunting familiar volumes, he can quote them
More eloquently than the men who wrote them,
Because he adds a private overtone
From old associations of his own.
A four-line epigram by Francis Quarles
Glows with the winter sunset on the Charles,
Pale rain in Pomfret shimmers through Jane Austen,
Through Trollope blows the salt east wind of Boston,
And Gibbon's wit was sharpened all too well
As Europe at Versailles declined and fell.

The notion that old books can be bewitched
By aspects of a life they have enriched
Might strike the casual reader who pursues
Detective fiction down a maze of clues
As somewhat morbid—yet I find it more so
To read all night about a missing torso.
And the new critic, happy jargoneer,
Who makes obscure what once was fairly clear,
While literature, beneath his magic passes,
Replaces mirrors with distorting glasses,
Would sigh, consult his glossary, and then
Return to nineteen twenty-two again.

Ah, but some books, like those where flowers were
   pressed,

Indeed become a fragrant palimpsest.
Sir Thomas Browne, skilled Merlin of the mood,
My rapt and adolescent solitude
Evokes, with beauty made more beautiful
By blossoming from eyeholes of a skull.
Sonnets of Shakespeare, Sidney, and Rosetti,
Drayton's *Idea* and Spenser's *Amoretti*
Discourse of double loves, their own and mine,
With reminiscences in every line;
And manuscripts, both harbingers and mourners
Of too much joy, grow dusty in dim corners.

Gray-fingered druid shadows gather now
The mistletoe upon the Golden Bough;
King Arthur's barge and the Nicean bark
Rush with the wandering ocean toward the dark;
The awkward Don avoids one final fall
By leading Rosinante to her stall.
Unswayed by critics and by vogue undaunted,
I am content among the books I've haunted:
The oftener they're read, the more they give.
In them my cumulative past shall live
Until, our long collaboration done,
I melt in earth, they in the lexicon.

An Epicurean Fragment

As PART of an exploding universe,
Our bit of fragmentation might be worse.
Seated beneath companionable stars,
Small beneficiary of cosmic wars,
I must admire how well our atom split
When once the Scientist exploded it.

Aeons ago an overwhelming fission
Blew the existing order to perdition,
But luckily so long before my birth
I need not mourn the burst that made the earth;
And, furthermore, I shall not be about
When, aeons hence, our fragment flickers out.

Spared both the introductory detonation
And the finale of annihilation,
With snug millenniums on either side,
Through the brief pleasantries of life I ride,
Remote from the beginning and the end.
I must regard that bombardier as friend,
Who, on an impulse, pulled the switch—or cork,
And gave us Earth, the Seasons, and New York.
Should I myself face atomized disaster,
At least I've profited from one far vaster,
And trust that equal happiness befall
Those who will benefit from one so small.

A Thought in Time

ELINOR WYLIE fell in love with Shelley,
    Amy Lowell fell in love with Keats,
Byron posthumously does so well he
    Can hardly count his valentine receipts.
Die early, poets, if you would adorn
The boudoirs of young ladies yet unborn.

Nobody ever fell in love with Shakespeare,
    Nobody ever fell in love with Blake.
A poet must be Lancelot of the Lake's peer
    Yet perish young and fair for Beauty's sake.

I'm far too old myself, at fifty-three;
No one will ever fall in love with me.

(But hold! a saving thought, a ray of hope!
Edith Sitwell fell in love with Pope.)

Assembling the Family

As I walked whistling through the cemetery
That haunted night of fitful moon and cloud,
I found my forebears' ghosts were making merry
At my expense, an undulating crowd

From whose pale mist of faces some came through
And looked me over with sepulchral laugh.
I shook with anger, and my voice shook, too—
"Go back to sleep beneath your epitaph."

"Ha, ha! There speaks my temper, as I live,"
A young man said, taking a pinch of snuff.
Around him all the shades grew talkative
As though they'd lain in silence long enough.

A gaffer in a cloak of homespun eyed me
And said, "His constitution's of the best.
I gave him that; I had the Word to guide me
And kept my health—'twas all that I possessed."

"Oh, bosh, old Puritan," a fumy ghost
In flowered waistcoat sneered, "he has my gout."
"His eyes," a young girl murmured, "are almost
As blue as mine before death put them out."

"He has my sense of humor, and he'll need it
In these drab days," a matron chuckled. "Ah,"
A pale youth sighed, "my genius, had he freed it
From meter, would have swept America."

"He has my hands." "The ears are the best feature,
And they are mine." "I gave him all that hair."
"He has my wit, but not my depth, poor creature."
"Ah, the kind heart! I'd know it anywhere."

They cried, "He's plagiaristically familiar!
Though now we're dust and lie where time has flung
    us,
There's not one particle of this live Hillyer
We dead ones can't account for here among us."

I would not be dismayed. "Oh, yes, there is!"
They rustled nearer, hovering to know.
"What is it?" "What?" they twittered, "what is this
You have, that not one soul of us can show?"

"I'll tell you when I join you." So I spoke,
And, by sheer curiosity consumed,
They flickered softly into bonfire smoke
And the wan moonlight where they lay entombed.

Serenade

You can not hear me, for my lute
Is old, the silver strings
Are almost mute while rings the blare
Of horn and clarion.
But song so noisily begun
Ends with the players' breath;

When they are done and death untunes
The final tone they dinned,
The lute still whispers in the wind.

Tierra del Fuego

THE farthest country is Tierra del Fuego,
That is the bleakest and the loneliest land;
There are the echoing mountains of felspar,
And salt winds walking the empty sand.

This country remembers the birth of the moon
From a rocky rib of the young earth's side;
It heard the white-hot mountains bellow
Against the march of the first flood tide.

I lifted a shell by the glass-green breakers
And heard what no man has heard before,
The whisper of steam in the hot fern forest
And slow feet crunching the ocean floor.

I saw the slanted flash of a seagull
When a sheaf of light poured over the clouds,
I heard the wind in the stiff dune grasses,
But I saw no sail and I heard no shrouds.

To a promontory of Tierra del Fuego
I climbed at noon and stretched my hand
Toward another country, remoter and bleaker.

Folk Song

Now time has gathered to itself
    The lily and the rose,
To mould upon a dusty shelf
    Where no man knows.

Now all things lovely fail and wane,
    The tender petals close,
And in the dawn shall bloom again
    No lily, no rose.

Now from the garden of your face
    The lily and the rose
Are gathered to a dusty place
    Where no man knows.

The Marooned

I SHOULD have been prepared that solemn morning
If God had given me sufficient warning
Such as He gave, I now surmise, to those
Far less deserving people. Well, God knows.
I told my wife, "There's thunder, the rain's coming."
And the rain fell and all day slanted drumming
Up the wide valley, such a plunging rain
As I have never seen and sha'n't again.
That night I played the prophet. "The wind's dropping,
The stars will soon be out, the rain is stopping.
Tomorrow all our fruit trees and our wheat
Will stand up fresh and glistening in the heat."
But I was no true prophet. Far from ceasing
The rain fell straight down steadily increasing

And day by day increased. Like spears it struck
My shattered fields and churned them into muck
And then a lake that drowned the orchard. Still,
We did not dream that it would reach our hill.
But as the days passed and it did not stop
At last we climbed up to the mountain top
With all provisions we could carry, while
Our house went floating past our little isle,
From which across the waters we could see
Dim shapes that sheltered others such as we.
But day by day they vanished, till our own
Amid the waste of waters stood alone,
A hundred feet by fifty, I should guess,
Though now it's less and hourly growing less.
And what I have to tell you next would seem
A mad mirage or a delirious dream,
Except that we both saw it. Otherwise,
We neither would have trusted our own eyes.
It was a huge, unwieldly barge that passed
So close we saw the knotholes in the mast,
A jerry-built affair, the shapeless sort
Of craft that children might have built in sport.
At first it seemed there was no crew at all,
But just a crowd of every animal
And bird you can imagine. One old man
Stood by the railing drinking from a can,
And when he saw us paused, and in a voice
Of thunder bawled, "O righteous men, rejoice!"
Then, when we shouted, shook his fist and roared,
"But you're not righteous! You can't come aboard!"
He danced a caper like a drunken clown,
Oblivious of the rain that hammered down.
Meanwhile, the animals all started yowling,
Grunting and snarling, whinnying and howling,

Bow-wow, miaou, chirp-chirp, and cockle-doo—
A crazy skipper and a floating zoo.
And when she got to windward—well, I wouldn't
Describe the smell, and anyway, I couldn't.
However, when we cursed, we cursed not that,
But being left to drown on Ararat.

Through the Drift of Years

NEVER go back: if landscapes do not change
Then the familiar will but seem more strange,
Shorn of the magic cast on field and tree
By memory's and time's mendacity;
Or, if they have changed, then we join the chorus
Who now, with their own recollections, bore us.
After a lapse of decades it is folly
To trace old joys through mists of melancholy:
The brooks we leaped so nimbly in our nonage
Are ditches now, or too wide for our tonnage;
And so with the dark-flowing past: one jumps
To drown midstream or sprawl in thorny clumps.

Not for a fortune (let me reconsider
If I am tempted by a generous bidder!)
Would I return to Paris, there to chase
Through haunted streets the phantom of lost grace.
To Denmark? Even northern beauties wilt,
Their golden tresses turned to gray or gilt—
Only their Mermaid by the Sound responds
Unchanged to memory, and she is bronze.
Boston—where everyone now hopefully looks
To find himself in one of Marquand's books?

No, I should be, beneath the State House dome,
Most homesick where I once was most at home.

Only New York is safe, where late and early
The riveters outstrip life's hurly-burly,
Where nothing now recalls my childhood era
That shook in needless fear of poor Cevera,
And witnessed Admiral Dewey's victory march
Pass by forever through the Dewey Arch.
I speak of childhood, but, to tell the truth,
There's nothing much remaining from my youth,
Hardly one stone upon another. Splendid!
Here all things change before they need be mended,
And mortal years, in contrast to such haste,
Move almost to immortal measures paced.

The Dance Will End at Midnight

UNDER this city
Slumbers another,
The houses of wattle
Standing on spiles.
Dark lake water
Deep as a nightmare
Stretches for ever
In midnight miles.

Under that city
Slumbers another,
The cave of the hunters,
The bone-strewn halls.
The bison and reindeer,
Swiftly immobile,
Halt in mid-motion
On midnight walls.

Here in this city
The lights go black.
The floors and the pavement
Billow and crack;
And the lake and the cavern
Have called us back.

The Pavilion by the Sea

THE white pavilion by the surf
Is delicate as paper lace,
Set in its little park of turf,
Inevitably out of place.

Here in the dreamy afternoons
While heat dissolves the world outside,
Cool as cloud-shadows in the moon's
Pale driftway, waltzers wheel and glide.

The chamber concert starts at ten—
Vivaldi, Monteverdi, Lully,
A little Mozart now and then,
All noted and applauded duly.

At stroke of midnight, fan and scarf
Are gathered up; goodnights are bowed;
While through the open doors, the surf
Pounds nearer, mercilessly loud.

This side the eighteenth century,
No lights more gently flow to dark
Than those that fade out by the sea
From the pavilion in the park.

Nocturne

OVER the cold hill the half-sun burning
Dull in its embers, and one leaf turning
Slowly down air; the white winter nearing
Through black frozen hours, long hours before
    morning;
The dead dark coming, the cold heart yearning
For home, for that room safe walled from the warning
Of the death beyond dying, the fear beyond fearing—
But look! You are loved, you were missed from the
    room,
And someone with a lantern is coming through the
    clearing,
Someone with a lantern on the path toward home.

Crèche

LIGHT grow longer, dark grow less,
Heart be strong in great gladness.
Shineth Tree and pierceth Star
Where the three archangels are;
You shall know them by their wings,
And, below them, three wise kings,
And afar, where endeth night,
The incarnate Child of Light.
Maiden holy, she attendeth;
Shepherd lowly, he befriendeth;
Oxen, sheep upon their knees
Guard the sleeping Prince of Peace.
Where the Gift is given again
We uplift our hearts. Amen.

THE DEATH
OF CAPTAIN NEMO

The Argument of the Poem

CAPTAIN NEMO, his submarine yacht, and the oceanic grotto on the volcanic isle are familiar to the reader from the pages of Jules Verne's *Mysterious Island*. There is no further similarity between Verne's excellent fantasy and the present work.

The time of the action is three days in the autumn of 1945. Two war-weary American poet-sailors are navigating their sloop to the East Indies. They have stopped off at the volcanic island where Nemo's submarine is moored. The poem opens on the day of his death at the age of almost a hundred.

The first section of the poem serves as an overture. The next six sections trace a fragmentary account of Nemo's life through passages from his Journal: his fatherless boyhood in the little chateau by the river Cher in Touraine; his dreams of wealth based on an ancestral chart showing a Spanish treasure ship; his exiles and travels; his meeting with a nihilist involved in the assassination of Alexander II of Russia; and, after the Franco-Prussian War of 1870, his conviction that the decline of European civilization that began with the French Revolution will continue to the end. Despairing of peace, he locates the treasure ship, and, thus enriched, constructs his submarine yacht, the *Nautilus*.

The guiding love of his life is a lady he refers to merely as the Princess. His physical encounters with a peasant girl end in ironic disillusionment. For some years he is under the malign influence of a woman of occult powers whom he calls the Witch. These figures, rising from the pages of the old Journal, haunt the thoughts of the two young sailors.

In the eighth section, the two sailors, according to Nemo's instructions, sink the *Nautilus* with Nemo's body lying in state in the main cabin. Thereafter the volcanic island explodes, and the young men set forth in their sloop.

The ninth and last section, until the very end, is a monologue by one of the sailors as he lies on deck while his companion is asleep below. At the end he is aroused from his revery by the companion.

I

In the festooned cave, the vault half undersea,
O sea nymphs garlanded with seaweed, weaving
Your watery paces among white stalactites,
Weave also now your song. Make with your music
The fields of sunlight. Sing *La Beauce en fleur*
And the brown vintners plucking the grapes of Time.
Sing of the rivers, the Cher rippling beneath
Gray arches, Diane de Poictier's Chenonceaux,
Where the cold, hooded hearths gape open skyward,
And salamanders keep their unwinking watch
Among the ashes of long burnt-out loves;
And by St. Avertin rippling where willows
Whisper beneath the drooping moon a hint
Of dying and of grace; sing of the Loing
That murmurs words the shadowy canals
Have lost in centuries of silence under
The dark forest of Fontainebleau. Sing boyhood
In that lost land.
                    For the old man lies dying.

In the festooned cave, the vault half undersea,
Sea nymphs among the stony moss and intricate
Stone roses, wind-flowers, pale anemones
That bloom for ever; sweetly singing nymphs
Weave with your music the bright fields of sunlight
While he lies dying in the far-traveled vessel,
The harmless submarine, which in the depths
Wound like a thought in a philosopher's mind
Among the crypts of everlasting change,
Until it came to rest in the watery grotto
On the volcanic island. The low arch
Of the grotto, framed in halted floods of lava,
Rumbled to the sluggish tide while the boat came gliding

In, far in, to the uttermost midnight mooring
And anchored dimly glowing, as last thoughts dimly
Glowing fade in caves of a midnight brain.
Soon he will travel again down rivers rippling
Among the willows, to sink away in grace.

Lure him in sweet delirium; the dying
Brain flickers with phosphorous beauty: boyhood
Bounding uphill to a grove of twittering aspens,
Where from the top he looks to another summit,
And beyond to another where beyond lies Paris,
The Princess, the Court Ball, the theater curtain
Rising to show a ballet by Delibes;
Then as the swan flies, as we measure distance
Between the song and death, a flight of clouds
Wings over weather warnings, darkens all,
Exeunt omnes.

                    In his later years
He had an organ on his boat, the *Nautilus,*
And played the black keys only, giving, it is said,
A Scottish melancholy to his music,
When his autonomous fingers still remembered
The thoughts that mind had sealed and heart had frozen
In amber to benumb the sting: wan battles,
Collapsing palaces, hysterical women
Torn from the pages of Euripides;
Boyhood betrayed; youth maimed; love, loyalty, murdered;
Chaos roaring above the calls for peace,
Till, with no backward glance lest hope betray him,
He dived deep down.

                         But what are these dreams of dreams?
These memoirs of a life he never lived?
Where was the land where no one had a name?

In most familiar confidence he was
Most reticent. All was anonymous.
The long life's code, deciphered in his heart,
Came from his lips like mediæval Latin
Illuminated with so intricate flowers,
All scrolled, all golden, and the letter lost.
And yet his undersong was gay, a half-heard
Harpsichord beneath the organ music,
More French than Scotch, more Renaissance than either,
Elizabethan Renaissance, perhaps,
The Gothic vault sealed with the Tudor rose.

Most mothered man, who had never known a father
Except as a bugle call by a long-closed grave
When the white daisies shone like daytime stars
Beside the river solemn beneath the willows,
Telemachus he was, yet no one told him
His father's tale of Ilium and the Isles.
Seeking his father he came to his life's close
Far off from all emotion except one:
Pity, a cold pity, devoid of tears.
But if his heart was empty, consider the riches
Stored in the foundering brain.

                         The old man stirs.
He sighs, the living glow goes out of his hands
Waxlike along the sheet, like the waxen hands
Of the mechanic chess-player worked with wires
By an old champion hidden among the draperies
And guiding the play in mirrors, long ago
In the famed Eden Musée. Consider the learning
Lost in this death, the music stored in the nerves;
The languages, long Latin, fibrous Greek,
And modern tongues in the minor key of love,
The nightingale singing by cloudy tides—

What was the use of the years shaping experience
Stored in so perishable a coffer? Why
These exquisite manners so unmannerly ended?
Grief will not rain on this so fertile death
The tears that water sapless blooms of ghost-land:
Pale wreaths that, when the mourners all are gone,
Stand fingering the air at dusk to frighten
The children amid the scuff of fallen leaves
And bonfire smoke. For this death only pity
Shines down like one star too far off for naming.

Now the last breath pencils the flaring nostrils.
The jaw drops. The eyes go out like sparks.

II

"Gravely I say to you, my mother, you have
Deserted me upon this Norman hill.
I am a foundling left at my own doorstep,
The foster-parent of my childhood, old
Before my time. I sit and watch the ships
Outbound against the dazzling afternoon
And say, 'Whatever I have wished to do
Must be postponed.' Some other incarnation
More fortunate will set me in the picture
That hangs beneath the sky, the bright confusion
Framed in its frame of sunlight, showing less
Of earth's intent than man's diversity,
And both somewhat obscured by the beholder."

Shall I read on? The notebook is not private.
The dead have nothing private but their tombs:
Have I not held the south wind in my hands,
And worn the heart of John Keats on my sleeve?

Come now, I'll read this manuscript—you, too,
Over my shoulder. Ghosts do not walk these years.
"More man's intent than earth's diversity."
The line has changed. I did not read it so
One moment thence. Words, meanings, manuscript,
All, if we do not watch with jailer's eyes,
Slip from their meanings and reverse their tracks.
Begin again:

        "Truly, my father, you have
Left me a chart showing where treasures lie
But marked no compass points. The galleon sank
In a lagoon to windward of the reef;
Your grandfather had it from his grandfather,
But whence the wind came that soft afternoon,
Which way the wavelets over the sharp coral
Were ruffled, no man knows. The parchment served
To mystify my boyhood, and a sonnet
I scrawled along the margin won my first love
Among the formal bric-a-brac she cherished
More than her dainty husband. 'Break his heart?
What nonsense! Careful there, that Sèvres medallion.'

"How many volumes of the lives I've noticed
Are stacked unwritten on the shelves. By moonlight
I take them down and read. As a child seeing
His first play shouts a warning to the hero,
So, in the spectral light, turning the pages,
I would unwind the past and wind it up
Another way: 'Do not wait there, dear Charles,
Just at the bottom of the stairs at tea-time;
You'll hear that witty friend telling your wife
Some reconstructed half-truth from your past.
Move out of earshot, just a yard or two,
And you and she will walk in linked contentment

Always; she does not mind; she will forget
Unless—ah, it's too late: the mad denial!'

"So have I walked about a vanished landscape
And rearranged the accidents, yet knowing
All was inevitable, if not then
And by those means, still by some other flaw
Picked at by fate until it cracked the heart,
And, perhaps worse, the noble bric-a-brac.

"With confidence, I could have been an artist,
But the age I inhabited said No;
Or walking in the wood I might have followed
Arthurian roads that end by a wild seashore
Where, when death struck me, the assuaging barge
With the three dolorous queens would bear me westward
Unto that other island, where no earthly
Treasure lay, but the triune peace of God.
Now, with my chart in hand, I turn away
From prospect of such poverty, compute
Pacific miles, provisions, cost and hazard:
The galleon lies in one of five lagoons
To windward of the reef. With so much gold
I can outbuild the chateaux of the Loire,
Move in a caliph's dream from hall to hall
Where lamps and perfumes hanging in the gloom
Vie with each other's softness till the eyes
Breathe sweetness, and the nostrils feast on color;
Where love dares not speak openly of age,
Nor even mirrors sharpen to the truth.
It lies to windward. Which way blew the wind
That August day three hundred years ago?"

Here let us pause and light a cigarette.
The question's answered by the circumstances.

Whatever was to be found, the old man found it,
But somehow, affluence did not please; perhaps
His audience was not worthy of his splendor,
Or else the clutter of magnificence,
That makes a man accessory to things,
Palled on him. Nothing but a treasure ship
Weighed down with Indian wealth could have arisen
So phoenix-like more glittering than itself
As this deep-diving yacht is to the galleon.
Here float the chateaux packed into one vessel,
One hermitage, and soon (we'll not deny him
His final word) sarcophagus of light
It will go down unfathomably, fading
From glare to glow to glimmer and to blackness.
So sink ambitions, even solitudes
That in the end are more vainglorious
Than all the ambitious glories of the world.

"Euripides saw Athens sail away
From the Piræus, watched Alcibiades,
No longer young, but plump, and with thin hair
And too long mimicry of boyhood, urge
Athenian youth as it embarked for ever
For Syracuse, the fever-haunted marshlands
Of Sicily, whence no more they should come
Unless their ghosts along the rotting wharves
Weep as they ask each other, 'Where is Athens?'
Well may the ghost of Athens ask where they are,
With spent eyes gazing ever out to sea.

"At midnight, I who write this fled Sédan
And saw the Germans on their way toward Paris.
I thought how Aristotle taught one conqueror
To deal more gently than a conqueror would
With worlds that clasp his feet. But this is no

Aristotelian mind, not Alexander,
But someone else, some conqueror from the steppes.

"Princess, the curtain does not fall, but see
The stage is empty; they have all departed,
The dancers and the music. May I go?
I would surmise the Orient is upon us;
Not Buddha, not Confucius, Lao Tze,
But Genghis Khan with all his commissars.
Princess, we are in the wrong part of the city:
Take my advice, don't try to reach your home
Tonight, wait here until another century,
Another incarnation. Meet me there."

III

The old man lies in state. The candles burn
Bright in the cabin of the *Nautilus*.
His face is sharpened to a white denial
Of violence; it turns toward history.
Moscva, the mad musician of the island,
Plays organ voluntaries, while the candles
Slanting their light, play life across the features.
A heavy pall of purple velvet hangs
Behind him; in embroidered gold, thrice lettered,
Nemo: Nemo: Nemo:—Thrice Nobody.
What claim has zero on a number? void
On velvet, anonymity on name?
Or was the old man (for he had the pall
Prepared) jesting, or did he find a pattern
In three times Nemo where one made no rhyme?

The water in the cave, heavily breathing,
Gives but an oily hint of storm without,

Which can be seen stuffing the arch with darkness
Where the cave opens to the sea. Let us
Go face the storm. My heart amid such pallor
Fails; I have never learned to love the dead.
As if invoked by Virgil, swirling voices
Howl and shout and die away in wailing;
The breakers stamp down on the beach together
Making the island shudder; chaos racing
The wheeling globe wins to the westward, dragging
The night behind on streamers of torn cloud.
I have seen storms too many, wars too many;
Bring out the old notebook; we can find a shelter
In things long past under the yellow dune,
Where sand is piled like hours that have run out
In broken cones of time, where winds are still.

Who is the Princess? she is hard to follow
Drifting along these waves of faded writing
As though from Astolat.

                    She was called Mathilde
Perhaps by error, for the name's erased,
And Blanche and Ruth—perhaps she had many names.
She was inscrutable, aloof, correct;
She would have graced a modern Court not often.
Here is her miniature, you see her face,
Eyes far apart, pale hair, and level brow;
You see the vanished gardens of Touraine
Where she would walk between the naked statues
A woman never to be thought of naked
Even in fantasy. She turns with half-smile
Acknowledging your bow, and so she passes
Down the clipped path, the colonnades of Love,
And where the lake laps on the marble wall
Steps down into her barge, is borne away

To dine with Flaubert in the lotus garden.
But there's no comedy in empty theaters;
The Princess, cloaked from head to foot, goes home
Alone, disdainful of the fear of thieves
That stalk the ill-lighted alleys. In her room
She yawns, flips pages of book after book,
Dante, Gaboriau, de Musset, Staël,
Goes over to the piano, strikes a note
Too loud for that thin night, and closes down
The instrument as though it were a coffin.
It is amazing how she puts off sleep
When there is nothing left to keep awake for;
All the suspense of something going to happen
Still teases her imagination though
It has no form; she is in love with nobody—
How the word echoes through the private room:
Nobody, nobody, nobody. Panic-stricken
She looks into her mirror to make sure
The one survivor of her world's still there.

All that is from the notebook. It goes on:
"Do you know Dürer's 'Knight, Death, and the Devil'?
I'll tell you whom the Knight is going to meet
When he turns off the road from Roncevaux:
It is his true love standing by the inn
Just at the goosegirl hour of twilight, when
The village pond is red with sunset embers.
She stands with arms akimbo, shrewdly blooming,
And every charm complete with counter-charm
For quick reversal when his whims reverse.
Her laughter shocks him and he reins his horse.
'Do you love music, doxie?' 'O, I am
Most skilled in music.' 'And do you play chess?'
'I am the champion of three counties.' 'Are you
Faithful in love?' 'That can I vouch for, surely,

Having loved none but you. I saw you pass
Once with your friends across the bridge. I saw you
Once with the Princess.' She observes the frown
And so defies it. 'A most pallid woman,
The Princess; better blood flows in my veins
As running brooks are better than still ponds.
I see that you are melancholy-laden
With armor on your heart. Be pleased to drop it;
Safe in my bed your heart needs no protection.
That helmet, too: ah, why should thought so shining
Be nullified behind lack-luster gold?'

"Then from the hills the Witch summoned me back.
I, who loved Paris, and could bathe more coolly
In dust that sang of the Ægean Sea
Than with a rout of mermaids at Ostend,
Half-Greek, half-modern, I was snared like rhyme
In a refrain by mediæval minstrels:
'The Princess and the Goosegirl and the Witch.'
There is a notion that with railway trains,
Rifles and stock exchanges and republics,
Magic, both black and white, was sterilized
By caustic fact. Ah, but the sidelong glances
The stars in passing through the streets of night
Cast on this rustic earth do so beguile him
With Babylonian longings, ancient arts
Of love, that in the seventh house of heaven
The wine cups made of skulls clank round together
As the old toast is drunk among the dice.
For seven years she held my soul in thrall,
The enchantress of green night and feathery trees.
Where balm of Gilead perfumed the air
And the new moon drenched all the sedge with dew
She taught me loveless love that made me wan
At thought of mortal woman. I have heard

That after I had served my seven years
They captured her afar from her charmed circle,
Shriveled and snarling, and they trussed her up,
Impaled her heart, buried her at the crossroads,
And beat the ground down with the sign of the Cross.
But when the wind is from a charnel quarter
And wisps of pale cloud fret the evening sky,
On upland roads in her abandoned country,
'Nemo!' I hear her whisper, and her shroud
Flutters and rustles in the rising wind.

"Here I left off three years ago. Meanwhile
Another war has harvested this village,
Leaving the chimney-stalks and husks of houses
With a few windows lighted this blue evening
Of cold December rain. Beneath my window
Two passersby go splashing down the highway.
I hear their voices: *'Heureux Noël!'*
How the great doors swing inward! Holy myth,
That flickers in the sanctuary lamp,
Still quaintly kindled and persistent myth
Where, having lost his way in darkness, Truth
Leans down and reads by reminiscent light
Directions homeward, and is reassured.
The little love god lying fast asleep
Does not observe what all about him see:
How wide and white the winter stars, how near,
While the huge earth goes swinging on through space
Like that (I watch one raindrop fall). Like that."

IV

"The big white snowflakes sifting over Paris
Curve cupped in air like feathers of sea-birds,

Stipple the gray walls of the Louvre and wink out
On the black pavement. This bleak afternoon
The few who walk abroad, heads down, gloved hands
On hat-brims or upholding snug umbrellas,
Make haste toward home. But I am indecisive
And scan the lighted windows of my friends,
Wistful but not so pitiably lonely
As to mount stairways and assume my mask.
The Countess Diane McCarty in her salon
Welcomes yet younger poets as she ages
And underwrites their feuds. At Arthur's house
Malice lays waste the guests who are not there
Or take their leave too early. Henriette
Delights to sail half-way toward Cythera,
And there are others—praise the human heart!—
Whose goodness glows through clouds of stifled yawns.
In short, I miss the friends I never had.

"Through curiosity, as evening flowed
Between the misted lights of the shop windows,
I followed a small man clad all in black
Furtively down an alley where he wheeled
And beckoned me, and so we both descended
To a basement room, bare but for one scarred table
And one oil lamp which, as he turned it higher,
Showed his lewd mouth, flat nose, and slanted eyes.
'You are late,' he said, 'Czar Alexander's gone,
But where is Anarchy? Overruled as usual,
Just as we feared. The Czar is dead, long live—
Yet look!' and he unfolded an old map.
'Look here, and here.' Across five continents
His finger, the creased knuckles and black nail,
Moved steadily. It seemed that where he pointed
The names of cities disappeared, the boundaries
Melted together in a yellow smear

Spread over all the world. 'Can you foresee
The outcome and be patient as the mole
That blindly burrows down his tunnel knowing
By instinct when the turf is undermined?
My friend—But who are you? Who are you? You are
Not the one I expected. I have betrayed
My servants!' Quick my gaze pursued him. 'Gone,'
I said aloud, and as the lamp blew out
I was aware the window had no panes.
My warning is your warning."

                       There it stops,
And when we question Death, we hear time ticking.
For we are from another generation,
America, the country no one loves:
Whose people love all countries but their own,
Despising what they grasp. See how tiaras
Regret they are not twinkling on a peeress
In English boredom at an English court,
How women stir beneath importunate lovers
Yearning for France, how poets flee abroad
To cry *Ich Dien* among the ostrich plumes
And feed on boots, how mystic orators
Scream accusation from the slums, discerning
The lights of Paradise that gild the Kremlin;
While over all America fair fields
Are plowed in fury like the hapless women,
And then are blown away to hang in dust
A phantom map of farms no man would love
Down to the roots, and forests hacked and rotting
Rear sawdust mountains where the poisoned streams
Seek absolution from the indifferent sea.
It must be no one means to live there longer
Than parasites upon a dying host.
Holy America, who dreamed so well,

Folding her eastern over her western hand
In the slow clasp of peace, O it is time
For all her poets to come home again,
To claim her dreams from the retreating stars.

From here America and Europe both
Are dreams, and this volcanic isle still shaking
With birth, and we are dreamers who have found here
The epitome of a lost civilization
In this antique of France, philosopher
Whose own volcanoes, being long extinct,
Serene in snow-capped meditation rise
Above the kneeling sea.

                    Be careful there.
Only old men and nations should embrace
The Way of Quiet. Buddha and lotus looks
Walk strangely in our streets. Beneath his hand
The sky is lulled, but still I hear the surf
Pounding the outer reef, our pulse of the world.

No pulse, a ticking clock. What season is it?

Here or at home? There are no seasons here.
At home it is late autumn, autumn sunrise,
Filtered through haze and fiery colored leaves,
And on the sea it dazzles where the dories
Loom up half visible, and voices carry
Over the tide and gurgle of green shells
Along the ebbing flats.

                  Those are but symbols
Of homesickness, and if we drank a bottle
We soon could weep. But truly, every day

We saw them without seeing them. The dead
Must suffer thinking how they took for granted
The small things never to be found again,
Not through eternity. Do they remember?
Do distant reed-notes from our fields pursue them
With music of regret for long days wasted
And loyal love spurned?

                                    I flip these mildewed pages
And find young Nemo knew the same despair:
"The words 'Farewell, Princess' were on my lips.
We stood surrounded by departing guests
Noisy with weariness. She wrung my hand
And drew me to one side. 'As you have said,
We shall await another incarnation,
And yet I go with you, you stay with me,
You in my book of hours and I in yours.'
The lights grew blurred among the girandoles
And the huge shadows swayed from side to side
As I went down the stairs alone to darkness.

"Months after that, one green night on the desert
When the white stars like daisies in the grass
Seemed near enough to gather, I recalled
The seeress Diotima and her words
To Socrates. (A wandering man who loves
His books must make his mind a library:
Then he can read by starlight.) Diotima
Having described the love beyond desire
For mortal youth, revealed the ultimate love
That fastening on none, seeks out in all things
Whatever part of beauty may be found,
Till from so many fragments to the last
Secreted spark, the many shine as One.

"Then suddenly I shivered, I was aware
Of the long, never-traveled road toward home.
And with my eyes still on the starlit page
Of memory, I read from that same discourse
How Aristophanes conversed on love:
In the beginning of the world our souls
Were split in two, and through all life thereafter
Each half goes looking for the other half
And questions every gaze, 'Are you my lover?'
And that idea of half-souls, of reunion,
Moved me to think how one half was the man,
The other half his native country. Only
The exile knows the pangs ascribed to love.

"This desert where I yearn for France was green
Four thousand years ago. The lost Egyptian
Exiled from here cried to the homing birds,
'Is no one left who speaks the tongue of Egypt?'
And the Chinese poet, sent to a far province,
Thought of his friends and wept. 'In this dull place
There is no one to be called remotely human.'
By the waters of Babylon all men together
Sit down and weep. The many weep as One."

V

"In the monastery where Fra Angelico
Left his indubitable and shining proof
Of courteous excursions into Heaven,
A young girl lingered past the hour of closing
And was pursued by grim custodians.
But she had come three thousand miles to witness
The Coronation of Our Lady; wherefore
She fled up the dim stairs. In failing light

The Glory gave its own light. God the Father
Held out the clustered stars to God the Son
Chosen to crown His Mother; in the air
The Holy Ghost hushed Heaven with hovering wings.
In that suspended moment the guards entered
All clash and anger. But the girl escaped them.
The picture was in darkness. To this day
No one has noticed among kneeling saints
The half-hid figure of the shy newcomer.

"Was the rapt novice, lost to outer things,
Moved by devotion or by art to merge
Her own identity in what she worshiped?
Perhaps by both, like him, the saintly artist.
So pure a faith deserved a place in Heaven,
And let us grant her that rare miracle:
The union of these sundered aspirations
Toward God and Beauty in one flight of stairs.
Most rare, indeed, since first the Renaissance
Offered the homeless gods of Greece a shelter,
No honeyed-colored Parthenon, but ceilings
Whereon they could disport as amoretti
Blandly adorning art no longer Christian,
No longer anything but art for art,
As modern sensitives make fashionable
Discoveries of thrills left undefined
In Notre Dame de Chartres, thus condescending
Toward beauty of whose essence they know nothing.

"To be a Dante, one must know, like Dante,
The Ptolemaic plan of many mansions
Down to the last entablature, and even
That knowledge waits on loftier truths beyond.
To comprehend a work that moves toward God
We had best start with God and work from Him

Who holds the key to labyrinths of art:
That is the highest criticism. Meanwhile,
When Beauty parts with God, religious people,
In shocked conclusion that all art is pagan,
Contrive such sanctuaries as would blight
All but the plaster saints with paper roses
Who simper round the dim confessionals.

"Why so much letter and so little spirit?
The gods of Greece had dignity enough
And wisdom to resent the blasphemies
Of aftercomers who missed all their meaning,
Their Pity and their Terror and their Peace.
From Egypt to the spire of Sainte Chapelle
All rose in piety, and every stone
Marked where some artist had invoked his god.
The Sainte Chapelle, stripped of its screen and altar
Means no more than so many walls and windows
Emptied of their intention, like poor Isis
Behind museum glass, her blank eyes fixed,
While the damp northern air dissolves the limestone
And grain by grain the goddess falls to sand.

"But the real Isis walked abroad one night
On the Egyptian desert; I could hear
Her childlike lamentation rise and fall:
'O Quiet Heart, where are you? O my brother!'
Not understanding gods who die, she faltered
Along the sands, calling her love, remembering
The dark head on the pillow, and around him
Among the plans but lately cast aside,
The fragments of his sacrificial body.
She still is heard, still unconsolable,
Among the dreams of women mourning soldiers,
And soldiers questioning everything they die for.

Think you that one of them was glad to die?—
Go ask the God who cried out from the Cross.

"To ward off evening chills of loneliness
The hermit warms his thought with indignation,
Casting old evils on the flames, yet knowing
How huge the forest looms whence come the faggots.
The fire grows hot, but all is a mirage
Where nothing can be done; we run in nightmares
And slip back with our speed.

                A summons came
Across the desert: I could now return,
Not to my home, for that was sold, nor even
My homeland as I left it. Nothing remained
Of the old courtesy and grace of style
Which, since the people lacked them, they destroyed
Rather than take the trouble to acquire.
From windows of a gutted palace leaned
A row of harlots, chattering and drunken:
'See, now the poor enjoy the rich man's house!'
And in the street a child, clawing for food,
Examined solemnly a piece of canvas
Torn from a Titian; I could recognize
The master by his treatment of a hand,
One piece of the enormous picture-puzzle
Not to be reassembled in our time.

"I failed to find the Princess. She was gone,
Said one, to Amiens. She was not in Amiens;
To Tours, to Quiberon, to Avignon,
The length and breadth of France. Someone had seen her
In every village, or imagined so,
Or said so for my comfort. In the spring
I found myself walking by dim canals

Of Fontainebleau. One evening on the towpath
When all the country swam in misty green,
An alley of great trees stretched on before me
Like Dante and Virgil meeting overhead;
And at the tunnel's end the cooling sunset
Flared from a void framed by a Norman arch.
I laughed suddenly. Now there was nothing left.
Experienced, disappointed, mazed in learning,
I had at last, like one who rides all day
To find himself at evening where he started,
Alighted at the doorstep of my childhood,
Knowing with awe what any peasant knows:
'I am the Resurrection and the Life.' "

VI

Blessëd be islands when time comes to leave them!
In a few weeks we should have seen such things
As would have made unsuited to our fellows
Our everyday acceptance of the strange.
Last night I could have sworn I saw the Princess
Standing upon the beach as though she stood
Outside the theater waiting for her carriage,
Wan in the cloudlight of the drooping moon.
Her hair was smooth and glistered with small gems,
Her cloak was glimmering like a veiled cascade;
She stood so near, I could read *Oberon*
Upon the programme in her hand, and see
The sapphire ring she wore outside her glove.
This was her own dream she was standing in,
A phrase or two of Weber's on her lips;
To her I was not there, was yet unborn.
Just for a moment the subdued night noises
Of Paris in another age were with me:

The footsteps passing, tones of conversation,
The hushing leaves of unremembered summer,
The clop-clop, clop-clop of a horse's hooves
That stamped and shuffled to a restive halt.
I am still dizzy with nocturnal spinning
Against all time and gravity, back through
A century and half-way round the world,
Or else it was the world, not I, revolving.
If time and space are false, why then I'm bankrupt
Of all my natural wealth. Most beautiful
The Princess was, but dust should hold its own.

Perhaps she was some memory of Nemo's
Still hovering from his not yet frozen mind,
Like mists on cooling planets after sunset.
O, I was wakeful, too. Behind my hut
In the small wilderness of palms I saw
The vampire flushed with life-blood of the soul.
And yet what shakes me most is not the evil
But that I looked on it with natural candor,
As if to say, "There's something I have missed."
Wound up in witchcraft I reproached myself
For my long lack of ingenuity;
Something ineffable and foul leaped forth
From the last oubliette of my disdain.
And that's enough to say. I am quite myself,
Yet wiser, being kinder. Having found
Within myself these unacknowledged beings
I am well warned against all prejudice.

Nemo was more secretive in his writings
Than are these uninvited funeral guests.

Nemo and every man. Until last night
I did not know my tenants. Some I smile at

Passing on stairways, some steal in at night
To make a carnival of sleep, but these—
Now you are laughing. The whole thing is boyish
Almost to affectation. Yet it's true.

I am no doubter, but the crystal morning
Is all washed clean in penitence and tears;
I'm for reality when it's for me,
And the real world is good for the time being.
Tomorrow morning, then, farewell to Nemo
And to his wistful book. We'll leave it with him.

But pry a little more.

                    We had been wiser
To start at the beginning and read through.
But listen: do you think he overheard me?

"We live in secret, Nemo and every man.
I am all men that live. I am your eyes
Who read these lines, yet am I Nobody.
Along the sliding stars from thought to thought
My being moves, yet when you see the starlight,
The star itself is æons on its way.
We live in forethought and in afterthought;
The present is a gaping void between.
All things are past before we know or feel them,
The keen blade cuts before the pain, we dwell
In memory, and that abyss between
Forethought and afterthought is not less deep
Than ages between us and Egypt, æons
Between the star and what we see of stars.
Forethought is the prediction of illusion,
Computing when the absent star will shine.

"When all computing's done, we reach that door,
Bronze, triple bronze to all the keys of science,
Where logic knocks with bloody knuckles raw,
And all philosophies claim keyhole views
Though no two make the same report; where faith
Waits for the host to swing the great doors wide
And knows that he will come. And he does come.

"Surely as all the rivers of the world,
Though they have various risings, various runnings,
And sometimes hide themselves far underground
Spreading in midnight lakes, but fall at last
Into the ocean, so after all our searchings,
Our curiosity and contemplation,
Man's reason ends, dissolving all its powers
In the necessity of Infinite power.

"Five hundred miles up the dense Orinoco
Yielded that single passage, and all else
Went drifting down between the jungles, waste
From undiscovered gold."

                          He traveled far.

What was the magnet?

                          The undiscovered gold?

He must have found that in the galleon—later.
Money and man seem never to agree
On the right time for meeting.

                          Give me money
And I'll arrange the happiest meeting.

                                        Yes,
So say the nations, and the battle's on.
To make the rich forget how poor they are
Makes others rich who furnish the diversions,
The wars, the concerts. Not much work is done
For natural need, food, shelter, clothing; mostly
We work to while away our apathy
And buy it back again, the price being life.

Is this the voice that told me of a morning
Washed clean in penitence and tears? Poor Nemo
Has squeezed your heart. Find me a livelier strain,
Timotheus.

                I can't foretell his pages:

"One thing we know of fate to each man's comfort
(And even the happiest man regrets some turning
On crossroads of his past itinerary):
Were we forevisioned with what every move
Would lead to, we would still from stubbornness
Or trust in luck or *deus ex machina*,
Go on in full view of the consequences.
What! will the maiden sour, grow foul, ill-humored,
Adulterous, deceitful, pandering
To my inferiors? I am as shrewd
As you; I also note the sprouting faults,
But love like mine can stagger prophecy,
Transmuting to some yet quiescent grace
Her lewder possibilities. She'll flower
To virtues unperceived by all your omens,
Needing but my desire to plant them there.

"I seem to hear young Nobody once more,
Pleading the goosegirl's virtue to the Princess,

Who, with clear sea-blue gaze looked out the window
Into the sky-blue calm, the steady sky,
The steady gaze, unclouded both. 'I hope
All that you say will be what you will say
Twenty years hence.' She smiled. 'Were I Cassandra,
Hector were dead before my eyes. You seem
Alive with love enough to keep Troy burning
A lifetime and yet never be consumed.'
I answered, 'You have learned to speak in riddles
Since my good fortune canceled our farewell.
Do you juggle symbols, poems à la mode?
Is this some idiom of the ateliers
Now that there is no Court?' 'I am not Cassandra
Nor Sappho nor the Sphinx. All I would say
Is simple, but it must be well concealed,
Something to be unwrapped when I am absent—
Years hence, perhaps. What are you asking for?
Do you know what you are asking for? My pride!'

"Years after, when her meaning was unwrapped
As she had said, and solitude at last
From shipwreck of my misadventured youth
Had salvaged wisdom and some gold, I told her
That now I understood. Was it too late?
Far-traveled and alone, I clenched the air
With lungs that breathed love's first full fiery breath.
Standing upon a cliff in Tierra del Fuego
To a dead woman I addressed my lovesong.
I write it now; I tell my future self,
However much doubt may bestride my view,
Once I saw clearly through the face of darkness
And looked into the face of light: My Love,
I have written prothalamions and sonnets
Each with its pleasurable fugue to hymn
The goddess and the harlot fleshed in one,

Dramatic scene, illusion, vanity,
To be dispelled by the least passing thought
Of how you twitched your veil before the mirror
Or poured the coffee. I once watched intent
While you drew on your glove, preoccupied
With the smooth fitting of each finger; then,
Spreading your hand, you looked up with a smile,
And we set out. It was a summer night,
The opera was Weber's *Oberon*.
Quite without warning, when the curtain fell,
You looked full in my face. 'If you don't love me,
Then I have wasted ten years of my life.'
And a perversity still unexplained
Froze me with panic. I said not one word.
The moment held its breath. You touched my arm:
'Please see me to the door and leave me there;
My carriage will be waiting.' 'Leave you there
Alone and unattended?' Ah, my Princess.
'Alone, perhaps. Attended by my thoughts
And by my servants. Isn't that enough?
Am I not lucky to have thoughts and servants?
Goodnight, dear friend.'
                              That is my song of love."

VII

"In the hall of the house which I once called my own,
I stood with the wind, another trespasser.
It came through the doors that opened on the terrace
And brought along the sough of the sighing pines.
The house was empty; those who had bought it from me
Had wearied of dark pines that grew so tall
And the little lake that froze to winter silence
And chattered the summer away through the dripping
    culvert.

It was late March, the wind was wild but warm,
The house like a ship in heavy seas responded.
As I entered a shadowed room I saw on the door-frame
That stood out golden caught in a streak of sun
The pencil lines that marked the growth of a child,
Each year the height and date scratched in the woodwork,
And then I knew my heart would never break.
I looked down from a window: all was gone
In wastes of weeds, the vineyard, the rose-garden;
So I turned from the house with freedom and relief,
No longer the custodian of decay.
I was satisfied; there was nothing more to do;
I must go from there and this time go for ever.

"In Brest I discovered a ketch, the *Antoinette*,
She had been a fisherman and then a yacht;
Now in the gay green sunlight painters and carpenters
With song and blasphemy renewed her youth.
Paint-brushes slapped her sides, hammers clanged over
The bay and echoed against surprised gray houses
That stood on stilts in the wash of the little inlet.
The *Antoinette* should become my privateer
With letters of marque to chase to the farthest horizon
That rakish vessel *Contentment* and make her my prize.
I had a crew of five, excellent Bretons,
Who hated everything, themselves included,
But most of all the sea, who fawned upon them
The while she lay in wait to drown her lovers.

"My *Antoinette* was solid, and she sat
Plump upon the water like a swan,
And like a swan's neck her most gracious bow
Curved to the bowsprit. *Splendor* is the word
For any ship we love. A sailor knows
My ship already, and one who does not know

Would but become entangled in the rigging
Of my description. Let him see her then,
A black, two-masted vessel leaning taut
Along the wind, close-hauled with gleaming sails,
The blue sea cresting white each side her prow,
And sea-gulls balancing the composition—
Is that the way to paint sea-pictures? Follow
Her course eight months; the sails become moth-color,
The black hull whitens with the brine, her speed
Slackens with drag of barnacles; and see,
In the expanse of watery Sahara
Where pallid clouds unmoving as the Sphinx
On the opaque horizon loom for days,
She lies becalmed, slow-heaving with the swell,
While the storm lurks accumulating fury.

"One afternoon a cold front menacing
As doom and laced with intermittent lightning,
Moved in across the sea, hung just above us,
Then thundered down like coal. We met with rage
The charging mountains and the purple wind.
They ripped our reefed-down mainsail while the ketch
Baring her teeth rose hissing to confront them.
We set a trysail, held her to the wind
And as the bow climbed up each murderous slope
I eased her off a little over one crest
To meet the next because we had to meet it,
Although each seemed the last. But *Antoinette*
Was fighting, the old forest in her timbers
Roared, cracked like cannon, threshed and shrieked aloud
Hatred to hatred, remembering old scores.
The sailors cursed the ship, the sea, and God,
And most of all cursed me, shaking their fists
As we surmounted one wave after another.
Yet, when the stormsail went, they had a second

Rigged and in place, bent like a pistol shot,
And every groaning line held to its utmost
Watched by ten Druid eyes. At last as night
Swirled down upon us and the storm redoubled
Maniacal, blind force, those seamen knew
Just at what instant by one hair of balance
I was to be relieved. One took the helm
Transferring from my tension to his own
With gradual hold the uninterrupted course,
And as I went below, the little ship
Fought on, her shoulders braced by Breton fury.

"Lying in darkness, up I mounted, up
Laboriously, lurched from side to side,
Then dropped as though the ship came down on rock
To grind and shudder there; then up once more,
The straining climb, and all my bones became
The framework of the ship, wrenched, pulled, and
          pounded,
My teeth set, and I wondered just how long
The contest could go on. The sea slid gurgling
Along the sides three inches from my hand,
And underneath bilge water to and fro
Sloshed in the well; the mast creaked in its step,
And overhead on deck big clumping boots
Stamped as though coming through. I think the hatred
Which made the Bretons masters of the storm
Came from their Druid forebears. The mad Vikings,
Seafolk for ever, fared forth with a shout;
But stocky Bretons thought of Druid temples
When they built ships, and with a forest curse
Repulsed wild winds and waves with magic wood.
In that Pacific wilderness I saw
A dolmen standing stark against the wind

On a wide plain rain-lashed and tenantless
In Brittany twelve thousand miles away."

Here he breaks off, and the next entry finds him
In China.

> How long after?

> > He doesn't say.
This is all piecemeal. Ah yes, here's the story
Written in retrospect: the typhoon wearied
Before the ship did; three days later found them
At anchor by an island, and he says:

"Since from the whole expanse of the Pacific
We had arrived at Somewhere long familiar
On an old yellow parchment, I conclude
That Someone had predestined us for Somewhere,
And the typhoon itself took on new meaning.
There were the five lagoons, concentric arcs
Within five reefs cradling the tiny island
With one small topknot of disheartened palms
That leaned one way from the prevailing wind.
To one side of them stood a single wall
Of what had been a fortress built of coral
And on a point a gallows-looking crosstree
From which, suspended like a tavern sign,
A metal plaque, bearing a coat of arms,
Creaked back and forth perpetually ill at ease.
We anchored off the island, went ashore
And from a basin of rainwater filled
Our few remaining casks. No one was there
Or had been for incalculable years.
The wind was steady from the east-southeast

And blew the heat out of the golden sunlight.
All the palms slanted from the east-southeast:
'It lies to windward.' East-southeast was windward
That August day three hundred years ago.
And there to windward lay in clear shoal water
A galleon all of coral, hull and spars,
Perfect enough to be a coral brooch
Shaped for the necklace of some giant woman.
Skeleton white it was with roseate shadows
Where the portholes had been and coral shafts
Where once had been the guns. My crew and I
Stared at the stony ship and crossed ourselves:
We feared there might be coral men below.
Barnacles first, I thought, to ossify
The wood and even the heavier shrouds and ratlines,
And then on barnacle foundation, coral,
To weld His Catholic Majesty's ambition
Into world history as the planet writes it.

"No doubt he would have been more gratified
To lay up treasure in a handier vault,
Yet he gained much in Heaven: before leaving
With all that long-sequestered wealth, we offered
Prayers for his soul, the first in centuries.
We sailed for China, landed at Foochow,
And there divided share and share alike,
Which, with the gift of *Antoinette,* brought out
More sun than ever shone on Brittany
From the five smiling faces of my friends.
They still were waving as they sailed from sight,
And maybe set a watch to go on waving
All the way overseas to Brittany,
Where, knowing *Antoinette* and seamanship,
I am quite sure they landed in due season.
Nor would they care what government the landsmen

Had set up as a scarecrow in their absence;
If they disliked new masters and new taxes
Or latest rats elected from the sewers,
There lay the *Antoinette* at anchor, there
Beyond all government the sea arranged
Pale sunset panoramas of delight.
They knew—as now I know—the only free man
Remains the one who never comes ashore.

"Yet who would choose vagaries of the ocean
Except in preference to those of men?
To escape all tyrannies there lie black fathoms
Where tempest can not pierce or passion brew
Its visible calamities. A sage
Whom I discovered by a waterfall
Counting the colors in the arch of spray
Through dynasties while emperors reigned and died,
Gave me a word to secret artisans
Who were his clan along the northern seaboard.
T'ang was their name. They could lay out a landscape
Of Heaven inside an agate stone, arranged
To fade out in the shadow and appear
Once more in sunlight; on the gnat-wing bridge
The tiny people bowed with folded fans
And smiled with sunlight greetings as though weather
Were chance instead of a huge hovering hand.
The T'angs delighted to outdo inventions
That held the West in awe, and with contempt
Break up the things as soon as they devised them
'And them it was the Son of Heaven called
To his imperial footstool when he needed
Their skill to chide a foolish Saxon Queen.
She gave him, to display her people's craft,
One fine steel needle, symbol of her strength
Tempered with delicacy. For three years

The clan of T'ang worked on the foreign thing,
And for three years the Son of Heaven labored
Shaping a poem. These are the sacred words:
Her cherished gift, steel needle fine and tempered,
The Queen bestowed upon the Son of Heaven,
Who with these lines returns the gift as worthy
Only of her who sent it. May she always
Deign to examine hidden truths in things.
Surely the needle is of steel, yet draws
A golden thought, the Emperor wrote. Inside
That needle the T'angs cunningly had shaped
Twelve smaller needles, each within the other,
A nest of needles growing ever finer
So that the last was hardly to be seen.
These are the artisans to build your *Nautilus;*
I have summoned the image to their minds already.'
"In later days I wondered as I cruised
Among blind creatures in the crypt of being
And prowled the dead streets of Atlantis, whether
This everlastingly nocturnal roamer
Were really I, Nemo, or if the rainbow
That hangs in permanent illusion over
The roaring gorge of time beheld two sages,
Old T'ang and Nemo with another name.

"In what past would you like to lose yourself?
For you may choose some day when all is spread
Beneath you, the green labyrinth whose paths
Mazed you from birth to death. Some day you will sit
Above them and examine the whole tangle,
Wrong turns, false exits, tricks that made you laugh
When you were young and all day lay ahead,
Then frightened you, then wearied you to death
As expectation failed, and night, too near,
Discredited all dreams that made you young.

Your pasts will all be spread beneath you, peopled
Just as they were, the settings all in place,
And here and there you'll choose an episode
That once seemed happy, but as knowledge dawns
That though you may repeat you can not alter
One grassblade, one mistake, one consequence,
You will have had enough: 'Come, little Jacques,
Stand by the doorframe and I'll measure you.
Don't push up taller. There, I'll make the mark.
Two inches and a half in one short year!
And think of all the years to come!' The pines
Sigh in the rising wind. You have had enough.
It is time to try a new life somewhere else,
Perhaps to fail again, but not so hugely;
Or if as hugely, in a new adventure;
Or if the old one, you will never know."

VIII

All ready, there?

            All ready, there?

                        Hear Echo.

Hear Echo!

            Answer, Echo.

                        Echo, Echo.

Harken, she answers cavern after cavern
Between the water and reverberant walls.

Be satisfied, and let poor Echo rest
And set a good example to old Logos
Who talks back to Himself among the planets
Shaking reluctant syllables of life
That clung like bats of silence to the cave
Till He dislodged them scolding into sunshine,
Half-blind and wholly inarticulate.

But listen!

       Yes, I have listened this half hour:
It is the drip of water from stalactites
Into the ebbing tide, like a clock ticking
Or bells ringing or a thousand other sounds
Liquid and mournful.

       No, there is something else,
Some deep uneasiness among the roots
Of this volcanic isle.

       Come now, it's time.
Get in the dinghy, we have work to do
Aboard the *Nautilus,* close up the hatches,
Turn all the lights on, open the sea-cocks,
And let the dazzling catafalque descend.

You have the little book?

       Here in my pocket.
Years hence we doubtless will regret the scruples
That made us give it back to him.

       Years past,
We would have been too scrupulous to read
One page of it.

I read it all last night.
These disconnected episodes assume
A shape from which I learned what I'd unlearn
Had I the proper drug. We live at once
In simultaneous time unnumbered lives
That in the flash of our immortal moment
Spring to one unified design; we are
Like islands seemingly divided, yet
All part of one vast Asia undersea.
I tell you, the whole universe is only
One flash. Let there be light, and there was light.
One flash in darkness. By my thought of this
I master it. Some other time I'll tell you,
Now's not the time: that saying works both ways.
Here, take the painter, make it fast right there
On that convenient cleat. She may go down
Much sooner than the old man thought she would,
And I'm for safety.

　　　　　　　Don't forget the wine
He wanted us to drink to his farewell.
How still it is down here, how very still.

It's strange to find him lying as we left him,
Each finger curved in place, the mouth so final,
The angle of each separate hair the same.
Perhaps the face is sharper. One who loved him
Should have been here.

　　　　　　　There is no one left who loved him.
I'll wind the clock up, that will last a month.
You think the water will not flood this cabin?

No, on the word of all the T'angs it won't.
He will lie here as long as any trace

Of Nemo can avoid eventual dust,
And for a month the clock will tick and chime
To keep him company, hours warding off
Eternity a while in case he's lonely.

The clock will be the lonely one. Nemo
Has done with time. He is so far from here
He does not see me as I fill these glasses
And hand you yours and pick mine up and say:
"Farewell, we leave you with eternal friends."

This is a vintage from his childhood chateau
Beside the river Cher, you see the picture
There on the bureau, a sweet place it was
Among the vineyards.

                              When these grapes were ripe
Charles X was on the throne of France, since when
France has not had a throne worth speaking of.

They are very proud of that.

                                   Give me your glass.
Speak of his happiness. What of his boyhood?
What of his childhood days?

                              He had a friend,
A young Chevalier nameless like the others,
And from their boyhood till the time when love
Gravely divides young men for women's pleasure,
They breathed one air, together climbed the Alps,
Sailed for a year across Phœnician fields,
Shared prizes for their Greek hexameters,
And loved the image each saw of the other
In the first girl they kissed. Those days were happy.

Even in those days cobwebs on this bottle
Were filming it with years. The eloquent wine
Speaks after man is silent.

Happiness?
Yes, in that boyhood friendship. After boyhood
Happiness grew more complicated, dwelling
In expectation. It was happiness
No doubt, that kept him hovering round the Princess,—
She was unhappy that he shunned the flame.
She has been dead these many years, she died
Before his visit to his ancient home;
He scarcely mentioned it. "I shall not see
Except in fading memory, the dear Princess.
I recommend her to St. Chrysostom."
The goosegirl was more durable than that:
She got a poet in trouble, married him,
Took him to Paris, and having climbed as far
As literature would take her, clambered through
The bedroom window of an Irish earl
And kicked the ladder out from under her.
As Countess Diane she held her court in Paris
Just at a time when mercifully for her
Bad language and coarse manners were in vogue.
Immortal girl, she can not die.

A smile
Flickered the old man's face.

He knew his world.
Here—one more glass apiece and there's an end.
Our sloop is ready; long before you wakened
I went aboard and stowed our gear below.
And by tomorrow at this time we'll be,
With luck, well on our way toward Celebes.

Shall we close down the coffin?

                               As you will—
No, there's no reason to. Let him lie there,
There may be other mourners than ourselves
Whose presence we are unaware of, waiting.
Ah, here's the handle. With one twist the sea-cocks
Open just wide enough to let her down
Slowly, with dignity. Are all the lights on?

Gleaming from stem to stern.

                          All ready, then.
You hear that hissing? That's the air forced up
By water seeping in. On deck, my friend,
The *Nautilus* is sinking under our feet.
Get in, I'll row; you sit in the sternsheets,
I'm heading for that shelf of shaly rock,
An excellent point of vantage. Are you weeping?
Then I'll not hide my face.

                          The deck's awash now.
The amber lights evaporate through water,
Melting like moonlight in a wash of cloud.
Down, down they go, dimmer, now they are gone.
How dark the darkness.

                     Give me your hand. What's that,
That clang?

                  The rock seems shifting underfoot.
Feel it? The whole foundation's shuddering.

One long wave swirled along the surface. Hurry,
We must get out of here, the grotto's crumbling.
Quick or the entrance will be blocked. Come out!

No, but we mustn't leave the rowboat here,
We'll need it. Take the painter, I'll fend off
While you tow.

                    It's like running in a dream.

But we have gained the arch. The sun is hanging
Burly and bloated through a veil of smoke.

Dark purple background and the red-hot mountain
Like Fujiyama painted in bright blood
Against the night.

                    I'll look when I'm aboard.
Easy, just bring us up under her stern.
Now I feel safe again. Haul on the anchor,
I'll hoist the mainsail. Just in time, my friend;
Five minutes later would have been too late.

There's a fair wind to bear us out of range.
Volcanoes should remember they're extinct;
They're more convulsive than old men in love.

And more impressive. What a pyre for Nemo!
He'll think he's pulled the whole world after him.
The island is a giant of itself,
A lump of bulging smoke feathered with flames.
Huge bursts of slag and rubble blaze sky-high
Trailing their smoke.

                    The wind is dying out.
I am afraid we've not come far enough
For safety. Over there beneath the smoke
The ocean boils with white-hot lava; listen,
I hear the hiss of the indignant tide

And a wild wail—what is it?—like the hoot
Of staring owls among the cosmic rafters.
I am afraid.

           The wind holds, faint but steady.
We'll make it.

             The whole mountain's going up!
It's cracked from top to bottom, one vast coal
Splitting in two, the core of flame exposed
And raging. The whole mountain's split in two!
Stop up your ears! Put your hand over your face!

The sloop with dreamlike gentleness climbs up
An earthquake wave as tall as the collapsing
Heights that thundered splashing into the sea.
And now, as gently setting down the sloop,
The earthquake wave goes onward bound for Asia,
Gliding over the sea, it leaves us rocking
With the faint wind slatting our idle sails,
Fanning the night, fanning the empty night.

IX

You are a poet sitting in a garden
One afternoon with summer in your hair,
The Queen of England paces down the pathway
And smiles and stops to ask you for a rhyme.
She too is writing poetry, a sonnet
To speed unwelcome princes from her strand,
And royal policies through rhymed iambics
Can best conceal the purpose of her whim.
The Queen goes on, the poet shrugs his shoulders,
The interruption is a good excuse

For doing nothing but survey the garden
With summer wind and sunlight in his hair.
That was another Queen, another poet,
The Thames was silver and the age was gold;
Perhaps the rhyme was polished once too often,
And all the loving princes sailed away.

The happiest life among a thousand lifetimes
Finds me at sea prefiguring my course,
My weary friend is sleeping in the cabin,
I lie on deck at ease, my mind a stage
Where exits move toward doorways of farewell
Sweeping their plumed hats downward in an arc,
And unpredictable arrivals tread
The minuet that failed for all their Mozart.
Rock crystal yields to me the Vedic ruby,
The tall Plantagenet unseals my lips,
The mantel of Copernicus, embroidered
With dancing planets warms my lonely sun.
And evermore the breathing ship sails onward
Her helm lashed in the confidential wind,
The destination a surprise of daybreak
Not to be opened till I'm sound asleep.

There are degrees of darkness, there are shadows,
I can see something, someone at the helm,
But let my head fall back, and slip from Plato
To join a lovers' rowdy night in Athens.
The sea nymphs singing from the foundered island
Pursue my ship with melodies of foam,
And grim Odysseus grappling with his shackles
Thinks of his son grown alien with the years.
Weave once again, O sea nymphs, from the rainbow
Climbing across the sunny gauze of rain,
The rivers that meander through the meadows

Of all the earth to lose themselves in ocean.
Weave with your music the long summer twilights
When fireflies in the trellis wink and bloom,
The perfumes of invisible dominions
Of undergrowth outside the garden wall.
Sing how from embers of long burnt-out lovers
The bright Phœnician bird spreads out her sails
And bites into the waves with beak of bronze
Quelling them for the halcyon's flight tomorrow.
Always tomorrow calm will be the ocean,
The work accomplished and the song well sung;
The old Queen gropes along the path at nightfall
Through snow and cold and puts her curse on rhyme.

The little of the world I understand
Has come to meet me. We have gone full-circle;
Both empty-handed we confess that neither
Is richer for his circumnavigation.
The place we meet is in a leafless woodland
Dripping with autumn rain. We both had hoped
To meet some other character, some friend
In charity, who'd say: "I'll care for you
For ever; come, my house is up the hillside
Above the dank woods and the standing pools.
And here's an orthodox philosophy
To keep you warm, my grandma's famous patchwork:
Do take it, it will keep you snug as childhood,
Just pull it up above your ears and sleep."
But there we are, my shivering stock of knowledge
And I, the same as when we met before,
We turn our pockets inside out with laughter,
Then linking arms seek out the village tavern
And drink our wits away. Our argument:
That there should be a new tense given to syntax
Where present, past, and future all combine,

Then with such wealth of speculation, gather
Our nothingness together and depart.

I lie on deck, my hands behind my head,
And let the watches of the night go by;
The sloop is drifting with an oily motion
Smoother than wind as though the keel were drawn
By subtly-running underwater currents,
And all lies thick and quieted like chambers
Of human hearts when they have ceased to beat.

Wake up, you fool! I need you. Come below.

All right. There's no wind and there's not a star
To steer by if there were. What is it now?

What is it now? Look at the compass needle.
It's circling like the second hand of time,
Around, slowly around. Give it a knock.
No, it goes on revolving round the dial
Inexorably and steadily. It is
More frightening than speed. A compass, mind you!

Something to do with the eruption, maybe?
Some core of lodestone from magnetic earth
Bared by upheaval? Some electric chaos?
I am no scientist.

                Around, around,
North, north by east, north-northeast, northeast
By north—it sucks my gaze around the dial
As though I had been drugged.

                                We'll wait for sunrise.
Meanwhile, I'll go on deck again to see

If I can find one star. No, no, not one.
And I begin to think there'll be no sunrise.
A strange and almost pleasant giddiness
Spins me. I feel that I am being unwound
From endless swathings of light gossamer.
Perhaps it was not, then, the compass needle
That was revolving, but the ship herself
Swirling like earth amid a noiseless maelstrom.
The dark is solid. Ah, no, not quite solid:
There are degrees of darkness, there are shadows
Deeper than other shadows. I see something.
Come up on deck! There's someone at the helm.

Who is it? Who is at the helm?

There's someone
Who knows these waters better than we do.
Now can you see him?

LYRICS
AND SHORTER POEMS · II ·

In the Tidal Marshes

WHITE above the afterflare
The moon rides up the brimming air
Singing in minor key the theme
Of light as music in a dream.
Lovers lying on the dune
Turn from each other toward the moon
And feel a tide far mightier
Than mortal love mount up to her
Who drowns in her magnetic flood
Mere urgencies of flesh and blood.
This is the hour the dying pass
Without a sigh to mist the glass,
So gently the translation made
From shadows to the world of shade.
So one who walks alone will stand
With love and death on either hand,
Invisible companions, who
Though cunningly disguised as two
Yet in reality are one,
Love the flesh, and death the bone.
He walks and feels the spectres glide
Along with him on either side,
And closer draws, to ward them off,
His cloak of loneliness, the stuff
Of pride, the pattern of control,
To hold them from his naked soul.
The long boardwalk lies dim before
Across the salt marsh to the shore.
My brother Sea, how tide on tide
Your waters shift, while you abide;

From wave on wave, lost in each other,
Your undiminished voice, my brother.
My sister Moon, how ray on ray
Is woven your unearthly day;
From ever changing gleam and glister
Your constancy of light, my sister.
My father God, how thought on thought
Your undiscovered mind is wrought;
From love whose end is death you gather
Your everlastingness, my father.
This is the hour the heart discovers
How love is mightier than lovers,
And this the hour the dying pass
Through death and know not what it was.
And one shall stand upon the shore
And he shall ponder them no more,
But dive into the sea, and swim
Far out, and peace shall go with him.

The Ivory Tower

WHO knows through what mysterious tensions
        these
Strange pinnacles of personality
Are held in place? The crazy structure sprawls
Over a territory not prepared
For architecture. Here a turret sags
Into the sand; there, on a rock, one tower
Stands up beyond its place in the design,
And gargoyles counterbalance random shifts
From equipoise, or flying buttresses,
As late as yesterday, were improvised
Hastily over space to clutch a wall.

Some years ago this efflorescent structure
Could have been simplified, even rebuilt,
According to a modern analyst,
With low walls all of glass to gulp the sun,
And the interior plain as everyday.
But now it is too late—one column shifted,
One bit of tracery removed, yes, even
One tendril of this ivy vine clipped off,
And the whole delicately balanced thing
Would crash around our ears. It is fantastic,
But best left as it is. And, by the way,
I note it has outlasted all the bombings.

A Memory

SKIPPING flat pebbles over the dark pond—
One of yours flipped nine times before it sank—
We watched the ripples spread, round after
        round,
Until the circles broke against the bank.
We played until the sun set, and the dank
Mist, heavy with the spicy smell of fern,
Rose from the reeds and warned us to return.

Of lives that intersect, then go their way,
At last to lose themselves alone against
The shores of silence, our brief hours of play
Seem now the symbol: the bright memory fenced
With deep, oblivious forest, and condensed
Into one flash, one fragmentary scene
That skips the surface of the years between.

You had a decade left that afternoon
Before you were to die in the first war;

But deep within me, like a sealed cocoon,
The memory clung, for fifty years and more,
To open for one sudden flight and soar
Into this moment lost in time beyond
Two small boys skipping pebbles over the pond.

The Bats

THESE caverns yield
But vampires upside down.
Better the field or town
Than exploration such as this.
These creatures of antithesis
With webbed unfeathered wings
Will shrink away from our electric wink
Lest they be dazzled to the dark of things.

Through stalactites
Of lancets in reverse
Their muffled flights rehearse
A foray on the world of sleep.
These are our underdreams that keep
Our secrets from ourselves,
The lark become half rodent in that dark
Wherein the downward mountain climber delves.

Seal all, before
In ragged panic driven
These nightwings pour to heaven
And seal us from our natural sun.
Of two forbidden trees, there's one
Untampered with till now,
Where throng, with their inaudibly high song,
The bats headdown from roots that are its bough.

The Cardinal Flower

COLD and amber
the shallow water,
shadowed by hemlocks;
there the cardinal
flower in August,
rooted in pebbles,
smolders dark red.
There, I remember,
we two swam,
and clambered on wet rocks,
part of primordial
earth in the awe-struck
hush of late summer.
There we are still,
no doubt, to the harkening
shadow, our laughter
braided through brawling
waters audibly.
That is the country
I never escaped from.

Visitants in a Country House
at Night

MY EARS are alert
For a sound thin as thought;
Fear strangles my heart,
And my nerves pull taut.

You are dead, you who loved.
("And you, too, are dead.")

Who said that? Who moved?
I will not turn my head.

Here where I centered
My life from one world
Noiselessly entered
Another, and swirled

Like mist in the air
When the air stands still.
Creak goes the stair,
Creak goes the sill.

Is that you, Walter Darrel,
Who died in the War?
Is that you, almost visible
There by the door?

Is that you, Johnny Wilson,
Who drowned in the sea,
Drifting upward from fathoms
Of darkness to me?

Is that you, Martha Fennel,
Your step on the stair,
The gun in your right hand,
The blood in your hair?

Peace to you, Walter,
On the hill at Verdun;
Drift back with the tide
Of forgetfulness, John.

Peace to you, Martha,
The bullet that tore

Through your brain was avenged
When he died in the War.

And your lover is dead,
He was drowned in the sea.
And I, too, am dead,—
All you once knew of me.

We were children, we ranged
Half in cloud, half in sun;
But now I am changed,
And you must be gone.

("Peace to *you*, Robert,")
Who said that?
             O deep
In the night, through the night,
Let me sleep.

Early in the Morning
(*En repos,* 1917)

EARLY in the morning
Of a lovely summer day,
As they lowered the bright awning
At the outdoor café,
I was breakfasting on croissants
And café au lait
Under greenery like scenery,
Rue François-Premier.
They were hosing the hot pavement
With a dash of flashing spray
And a smell like summer showers
When the dust is drenched away.

Under greenery like scenery,
Rue François-Premier,
I was twenty and a lover
And in Paradise to stay,
Very early in the morning
Of a lovely summer day.

General Galliéni

WHO now remembers General Galliéni,
Whose Paris taxicabs, one-lunged and leaky,
Charged to the Marne, just as the Kaiser's *veni*
And *vidi* were about to turn to *vici*?

Like herds of superannuated cattle
The lame, asthmatic vehicles stampeded,
Backfiring, honking cavalry to battle
With reinforcements just when they were needed.

Paris was saved; the politicians boldly
Returned from flight, but being none too partial
To Galliéni's methods, thanked him coldly—
And he was five years dead when named a marshal.

The vague, nearsighted warrior gets a column
In the *Britannica,* as one well fitted
To be a marshal, but the tone is solemn;
His crowning feat is scornfully omitted.

Joffre is remembered worthily, and Foch;
The fame of Pétain hisses in its embers,
But Galliéni, who nonplussed the Boche
With his embattled taxis, none remembers

Except where Roland in the Pyrenees,
Blowing his evening-echoed note forlorn,
Smiles, reassured, to hear upon the breeze
The answering honk of Galliéni's horn.

Departing Song Sparrows

FAREWELL, song sparrows of spring,
Pausing once more to sing
Before your southward flight
Your crystal song,
Leaving us to the white
Dream winter-long
Of your returning.
Beneath the hazy flare
Of autumn, fields are bare
Except for milkweed fluff
Adrift on the hesitant air
And the smoke of leaves burning.
Farewell, our season yields
To time. There was song enough
Perhaps, for with changing mood
We look to the silent fields
And find them good.

The Girl in the Garden

AFTER the long dry season
I look from the eastern window
Conversant with the dawn.
I will not speak a word;
My finger on my lips
Enjoins the leaves to silence.

Delicate is the morning,
The threshold of hesitant autumn
With no hint of farewell.

Summer was curled to a parchment
By drought and withering heat
That were deadlier than a winter.
But suddenly into my garden
One evening in the starlight
Came the lady, the sister of flowers.
She merely touched them in passing,
And they lifted up as though starlight
Had fallen as slanting rain.

The dawn of hesitant autumn
Spun from the dew and the sunlight
Reveals the unfading garden
In the country where I have dreamed.
Music attends her waking,
The girl who walked in my garden.
As the sun lifts up her eyelids
She will come to the eastern window,
And the leaves may begin their song.

The Scholar to His Valentine

MY LOVE "is like the melodie that's sweetly
Played in tune." (Burns put it very neatly.)
And I could easily quote, had I the space,
A thousand amorous lines of equal grace.
But scholars, when in love, must guard themselves
Against too great dependence on their shelves.
What say the masters of poetic art?
" 'Fool!' said my muse to me, 'look in thy heart

And write' " (Sir Philip Sidney, by the way).
And "rhetoric forsook him" (Thomas Gray).

Nevertheless, with Plato's approbation,
We have the advantage of imagination;
How else, my dear, to speak quite candidly,
Could you my Chloe, I your Daphnis, be?
Myopia, the muse of higher truth,
Preserves your beauty and prolongs my youth—
"Eternal summer gilds them yet" (Lord Byron),
Though gouty grows the swain and stout the siren,
And passion, suavely tuned to middle age,
Breathes its full fervor from the lyric page.

And furthermore, St. Valentine has chosen
This day when everybody will be frozen,
Both young and old, indifferent together
To any topic but the shivering weather;
When Cupid, barred from groves beneath the moon,
Must hibernate in poetry till June,
Though far from powerless. You would be astonished!
"Nothing refuse—" (So Emerson admonished.)
"Come live with me and be my love." That line
Was Marlowe's, Ralegh's, Donne's, and—deem it mine.

One Kind of Colloquy

HERE in the garden, strolling slowly
With a young poet who is wholly
Rapt in his own imagination,
I leave to him the conversation,
Knowing that through his golden mist
I'd loom, a sad materialist.

How creature comforts come to be
A substitute for ecstasy!
Wordsworth, romantic though he was,
Confessed how revelations pass;
And Henry Vaughan, light's own true son,
Observed the same phenomenon.
Blake moved in radiance to the end
As Catherine saw his soul ascend
Clapping its hands; and Shakespeare, after
Storming the globe's extremest rafter,
Vanished in more tempestuous magic
Beyond the comic or the tragic.
But, on the whole, the poets mostly,
Becoming less remote and ghostly,
Repeat with stresses more intense
Our general experience,
When dithyrambic dreams attract
Less than the fantasies of fact.
But why should I anticipate
This younger poet's future state?
He speaks of love that moves the stars,
Of revolution ending wars,
Abstractions realer than the real,
And, clear as crystal, the Ideal.
His nostrils quiver in response
To ethers that I savored once;
His thoughts like angels climb the rungs
Of ladders toward the gift of tongues.
How accurately he can spell
The name of the Ineffable!

Not yet acknowledging the birth
Of beauty from component earth,
He floats through flowers that yesterday
Were treated with manure and spray,

And sees them vaguely as pale gems
Suspended without roots or stems.
All air and fire, his darting sense
Spurns the two coarser elements—
Water, from which we first were born,
And earth, to which we all return.
Better for him to keep the rapture
That I have known but can't recapture;
Better for me my narrower joy
That views of distance would destroy.
On this bright lawn, this flowering slope,
Keats could have bared his soul to Pope,
And wit relived the age of hope.

The Hammock in the Orchard

ONCE more the hazy southwest wind prevails,
Blowing a vague mist over sea and sails,
And in old orchards indolently heaves
The unmown grass and filigree of leaves.
Deep summer drones a reminiscent tune
Through the long, languorous, hot afternoon,
Unveiling vistas of the past that seem
So real, reality becomes a dream.
It would not much surprise me to observe
An open trolley car lurch round the curve,
Or hear down quiet sidestreets the clip-clop
Of horses stumbling to a patient stop,
Or watch four-masted schooners Bangor-bound
And proud sidewheelers churning up the Sound.
It would not much surprise me if I saw—
As I can almost see—my aunt-in-law,
Recumbent in the hammock slung between
These orchard trees that still are hale and green,

Her mouth agape in unbecoming slumber
Over some novel or Midsummer Number.

A rusty hook protruding from the bark
Of this old apple tree preserves the mark
Of summers long ago—my own first twenty—
When Kirk Monroe, the Rover Boys, and Henty
Gave way to Dickens, then a somewhat tardy
And frowned-upon enthusiasm for Hardy.
I captured the fringed hammock, though, but seldom:
My aunt-in-law, a most voluminous beldam,
Invited for the weekend, would make tracks
As soon as lunch was over, to relax
Beneath the fretted shade with summer reading
Designed as an escape from sports or weeding.
While tennis players practiced the new Lawford,
George Barr McCutcheon and F. Marion Crawford
In Graustark or in Rome beguiled Aunt Jane
Until the thunderheads dissolved in rain.
Anthony Hope she worshipped, and was fond
Of William Locke's *Beloved Vagabond*.
Ah, and what stammered words and flaming cheeks
Betrayed her, caught red-handed with *Three Weeks!*

Except in Hardy and in Madam Glyn,
Vice was unknown to fiction's heroine.
While seldom tempted, never taking chances,
The lovely girl was trapped by circumstances
In which the villain was empowered to try
The extra squeeze of hand, the glint of eye.
The hero, literally a holy terror,
Soon thrashed him to acknowledgment of error,
Whereat he vanished, or, contritely shedding
His sins, turned up as best man at the wedding.

Poor folk were worthy and the rich were kind;
Humor was lame but lambently refined;
And sometimes literature became more ample
In depth of moral purpose; for example,
Problems for readers not too easily bored
Were raised and solved by Mrs. Humphry Ward.

Explore your attics and your mustier shelves
To summon back the era for yourselves.
Then while the shrill northeaster, blind with rain,
Drowns all the world beyond the windowpane,
Your ghosts will come indoors and reassemble
To read beside the fire. You needn't tremble—
They'll be too lost in *Allan Quartermain*
Or *Hugh Wynne, Quaker,* or the last Hall Caine
To note your presence, though perplexed a little
To find the leaves so mildewed and so brittle.
Only the shadow children, at the chime
Of the unfailing "once upon a time,"
Find wonderland behind the looking glass
And hear the winds among the willows pass
Over the jungle folk, the treasure islands,
Pale Camelot and Scotland's haunted highlands,
Just as they always were, for Time swings free
Before the whispered "Open sesame."

The First World War unleashed another age:
With *What Price Glory?* swear-words reached the stage;
With Michael Arlen and F. Scott Fitzgerald
The heroines set out to be imperilled.
Convention reeled before each brash newcomer,
And summer reading grew too hot for summer.
The hammock, weathered to a streaky gray,
Swung empty, and at last was tucked away

With *Little Colonel* books, *Monsieur Beaucaire*,
And Baedekers to towns no longer there.

Yet in the orchard where the grass grows high
And green leaves intercept the shining sky,
Dorothy Vernon steps from Haddon Hall,
Young Carthaginians breach the Roman wall,
Princes and paupers, sorcerers and thieves,
People the background tapestry of leaves,
And Life's long fiction, now so nearly done,
Is flicked back by the wind to Chapter One.

The Garden in Pomfret

THE starry music through remote
And silent evening slowly grew.
At first, white echoes note by note
Shaking the air they trembled through;
Then with a sharpened clearness born
Of growing silence to their sound
And growing darkness to their light,
They lifted patterns from the ground,
From silence shaped the silver horn
To blow the reveille of night
And ring the chiming globes of dew.

And all about me where I stood
Unearthly blossoms came to view;
Deep in the chancels of the wood
Pale crystals whitened two by two.
"A starry night!" I said aloud.
"A starry night," the dew replied.
Then from beneath my feet the song
Of earth streamed in a silent tide.

I rode the star of earth in proud
Replying light and bade the throng
Begin their silver song anew.

Lament for the Coasting Fleets

THE coasting fleets that not so long ago
Crowded offshore, propelled by sails or steam,
And gave a human meaning to the flow
And ebb of tides have vanished like a dream.

Processions of them used to dot the seaboard,
Now empty from horizon to the shore,—
Tall barks with clipper bows and lofty freeboard,
Gay summer pleasure-steamers by the score;

Schooners that Bath and Bangor were renowned for,
Gaff-rigged and low with lumber or with grain;
And fishing smacks, and coastal liners bound for
Dozens of ports from Florida to Maine;

And paddlewheelers of the white flotilla
That flew the flag of the Fall River Line,
Puritan, Pilgrim, Commonwealth, Priscilla,
Treading with plunging wheels the frothy brine:—

At twilight from my little sloop I hailed them
As they swept by me, towering tiers of light,
And left me rocking in the wake that trailed them,
Gazing after their beauty lost in night.

Fire, air, water, set the old ships in motion,
Three cleanly elements for steam or sails;
The fourth, decayed as oil, now streaks the ocean
With irridescent filth like tracks of snails.

The waves stretch empty that were plied for ages
By coasting vessels vanished from the world;
Pressure's at zero in the rusty gauges,
And on the spars sails are forever furled.

Light, Variable Winds

THIS is the getting-nowhere breeze
That tries the soul of mariners—
The reason that the Seven Seas
Are peopled with philosophers.

We come about or jibe, to learn
That wind can box the compass, too,
Adroitly turning as we turn,
Adverse no matter what we do.

Still, better than dead calm, at least
It does impel us back and forth,
Giving the west some hope of east,
The south mirages of the north.

Hardened philosophers, we thrive
On facts we cannot overcome
As in vague twilight we arrive
Where in vague dawn we started from.

Fog

TEMPESTS lift the sea, but their howling onrush
also nerves the strength in the hands of helmsmen
gauging slants of waves and the prow that climbs them,
    true to a hair's breadth.

Fog it is we fear, when familiar headlands,
wharf, and shoreside turf, and the village housetops
—smudged mirages—vanish, and vaulted ghostland
    closes around us.

Air and water mingle in seamless twilight.
Only near the hull there is liquid darkness
still discernible as a patch of ocean
    feathered with salt foam.

Cry of sea gull, clang of the lone bell buoy,
voices inarticulate blown from nowhere,
muffled chugs of engines from all sides haunt us,
    lost in the gray drift.

Chill pervades our bones, as though we were made of
fog ourselves; our hands are benumbed, our eyebrows
furred with wet, like eaves in the rain that blur the
    windows beneath them.

Solitude imagines a looming iceberg,
rocks ahead, or reefs, or a crazy speedboat,
or, in wisps of vapor along the fog bank,
    faces of drowned men.

Where is safe to head but forever eastward?
Then, not quite believing the hint of daylight,
first we feel a warmth and perceive a vague form
    sharpen to contours.

Fog and fear together dissolve in sunburst.
Number 4 red nun is abeam to starboard.
Ah, that landfalls could be the home-port always
    when we are fogbound!

Familiar Faces, Long Departed

WHERE are the dear domestics, white and black,
Who stayed for years or hastened to repack,
Diverse as weather, changeful as the wind,
And kind to children over-disciplined?
No more the stifled giggle on the stairs,
The scornful flounce when Madam put on airs,
The sympathetic heart beneath the starch
When boys who loved to dance were trained to march.
The subject round which every talk revolved,
The servant problem, now at last is solved.

The Huldas, Posies, Bridies, and Francines
Are happier as servants of machines.
Time-clocks have superseded bells, and wages
Climb with the pointer in the pressure-gauges.
The hands that knew such varied skills prepare
The lean assembly line's unvaried fare,
To make the things that serve as their replacement
In every function from third floor to basement,
And heartlessly supplant with a device
The youth who brought romance as well as ice.

The house is shaken with the whining hum
That Nature most abhors, the vacuum.
Freed from the mute reproval of the maid,
Talk has grown loose and manners have decayed.
Damask and fingerbowls are empty names,
At breakfast time the toast leaps up in flames;
The cocktail hour expands, the dinner shrinks,
Now no one needs to care what Bridget thinks.
All in prefabricated ruin lies,
And Ganymede gives notice in the skies.

"Seven Times One Are Seven"
(3 June 1902)

IN HIS grandmother's garden was a cake with seven candles,
And the family had foregathered that rose-haunted afternoon.
Aunt Jane was singing Jean Ingelow's effusion
About a seventh birthday to a sentimental tune.
"It's a birthday to remember," said his grandmother smiling,
"With all the roses out on the third day of June."

His brother said, "There should have been eight candles.
    One to grow on."
"For seven years," the Rector said, "I think he's pretty tall."
They talked about him amiably as though he were
    not present,
And he felt at his own party embarrassingly small.
His mother sat in silence, and he knew the scent of roses
Had made her think—as he did—of his father's funeral.

The books for his birthday had all been sent from England.
"No one writes for children like the English," said Aunt
    Jane.
"How about Louisa May Alcott?" asked the Rector.
"Only fit for girls," said his brother with disdain.
His uncle coughed and murmured, "There's *Huckleberry
    Finn.*"
"Good heavens!" said his grandmother, "that vulgar
    Mark Twain?"

Momently his birthday was slipping through his fingers,
Till, "Blow and make a wish," said his sister. So he blew.
Out went four candles, the wind blew out the other three,
And he was disappointed that he'd blown out so few.
His mother said, "How wonderful! Four sevenths of your
    happiness
Is way above the average for your wishes to come true."

The Rector and the members of the older generation
Put aside their plates and settled comfortably to chat.
His brother went to baseball, his sister to a friend's house,
And everything seemed suddenly quite commonplace and
    flat.
Freed from all attention now, his birthday party over with,
He chose a book called *Storyland* and lost himself in that.

Crumbly Court

THE peacock, herald in the dappled park
Where ladies strolled to greet the hierarch,
The noble house, half ivy and half stone,
Where scores could gather and yet seem alone,
The lord, the guest, the punctual servitor
Who brought the bath at eight, the tea at four,
Tutors and children, youths in tennis togs,
Gamekeepers, horses, solemn-wagging dogs,—
These, living once, are now but picturesque
Like yellow diaries in a long-locked desk.
Here where the poet walked to meet the matron
Who had induced her lord to be his patron,
The yews that made neat couplets of the border
Sprawl like free verse in meterless disorder.
Within the bell-tower of the chapel, Time
Evokes no answer from the rusty chime.
No visitors regard with bated breath
The bed where slept the great Elizabeth,
Or read the masques in manuscript whose names
Failed to outlive their lesser subject, James.
Here in this court the Master of the Rolls,
Falling to dust, crumples the crested scrolls,
While lord and lady into memory melt,
One with the Saxon, Roman, and the Celt.

Underneath Gray Winter Skies

AGAINST dull sunset, daily growing duller,
As winter freezes the last hint of color,
Black branches interlace in stiff despair,
As though they'd never known a kindlier air,
And I, in wool like any sheep incased,
Regard the wintry landscape with distaste;
Reluctant rustic, pastoral renegade,
I yearn for ostentation and parade,
Vast corridors, soft carpets, half-veiled eyes
Of sleek suburban matrons in disguise,
Vain, silken creatures—or, more likely, rayon—
And other follies satire loves to play on.

O doorman, twirl for me revolving doors
Back to the people I once shunned as bores!
In some discreet palm garden let me sit
With Mrs. Dowdy, plain and void of wit,
She whom in summer's pride I left to swelter
Glows in my memory as a kindly shelter;
Or in the bar, may Colonel Bland accept
My lame excuse that friendship overslept,
And blessedly unblest with brains or rancor,
Forget that I'm a bard and he's a banker.
Oh, nothing human's alien to me
Who freeze alone beneath a frozen tree.

Long, long ago, when the old Waldorf stood
At Fifth and Thirty-fourth Street (as it should),
I was a bold, imaginative child
Who liked my winters bronchial and wild.
To city ignorance of winter's malice
Shopwindows seemed the aurora borealis,

The hissing snow a summons to my soul,
The Waldorf a snug igloo near the Pole.
Could I with equal ease and more acumen
But change this blasted heath to something human!
Nature is indestructible, alas;
It is the cities that too quickly pass.

Elizabethan Pastoral Landscape

*Upon the setting of that bright Occidental Star
Queen Elizabeth of most happy memory.*

Is THE half-light on groves and flowery lawn
The harbinger of darkness or of dawn?
This timeless time in gardens starred with blooms
Freighting the wandering wind with faint perfumes
Glows evanescently where shepherds stroll
With lutes and viols, singing out their soul;
And, from the casements half concealed in green,
Elbows on sill, the young girls, listening, lean,
Their soft lips parted at love's budding hour,
Trembling to unfold, yet hesitant to flower,
As innocence, transported with desire,
Dreams of the joys wherein it will expire.

The birds confuse the hour, for every fowl,
From sunrise lark to nightingale and owl,
Phoenix and turtledove and dying swan,
Sings madrigal or prothalamion,
And busily the jocund cuckoo warns
Unhappy husbands of their sprouting horns.
Nor can the season by the flowers be told:
Grapes ripen with the rose and marigold;

And Bacchus, reeling by with drunken band,
Snatching at spring, finds autumn in his hand.
Then all the landscape darkens: Death goes by;
Beauty turns pale, dust closes Helen's eye.

Sing lullabye, my lady is but sleeping
While poets take her melody in keeping.
Once more the landscape glows as golden rain
Pours from the shattered galleons of Spain.
Borne on salt winds from desolate seas of ice,
Or sunburnt Indies or the Isles of Spice,
Like high sea-falcons homing from their sport,
Tall captains fold their fiery wings at Court,
To claim the smile of their mysterious Queen
Too dazzling to be more than briefly seen,
Whose final exit from this masque will mark
The gradual descending of the dark.

Elegy

*On a Dead Mermaid Washed Ashore
at Plymouth Rock*

PALLIDLY sleeping, the Ocean's mysterious daughter
Lies in the lee of the boulder that shattered her charms.
Dawn rushes over the level horizon of water
And touches to flickering crimson her face and her arms,
While every scale in that marvelous tail
Quivers with color like sun on a Mediterranean sail.

Could you not keep to the ocean that lulls the equator,
Soulless, immortal, and fatally fair to the gaze?
Or were you called to the North by an ecstasy greater
Than any you knew in those ancient and terrible days

When all your delight was to flash on the sight
Of the wondering sailor and lure him to death in the
    watery night?

Was there, perhaps, on the deck of some far-away vessel
A lad from New England whose fancy you failed to en-
    snare?
Who, born of this virtuous rock, and accustomed to
    wrestle
With beauty in all of its forms, became your despair,
And awoke in your breast a mortal unrest
That dragged you away from the south to your death in
    the cold northwest?

Pallidly sleeping, your body is shorn of its magic,
But Death gives a soul to whatever is lovely and dies.
Now Ocean reclaims you again, lest a marvel so tragic
Remain to be mocked by our earthly and virtuous eyes,
And reason redeems already what seems
Only a fable like all our strange and beautiful dreams.

The Gull

GRAY wings, O gray wings against a cloud
Over the rough waves flashing,
Whose was the scream, startling and loud,
Keen through the skies,—was it thine,
Piercing above the wind and the moaning whine
Of the wide seas dashing?
Whose was the scream that I heard
In the midst of the hurrying air,—
Was it thine, lost bird,
Or the voice of an old despair

Shrieking from years long dead,
Wild spirit flying
On tempest wings that passed and fled
Through the storm crying?

A Ballade of Revelation

MIRACLES cannot be produced at will—
I had no hint that lowering summer day,
High on the heather-covered little hill
That wanders upward from Katama Bay,
Of any exaltation, till one ray
Of sunlight touched me, and a thousand springs
Of life leaped in me from the dead who lay
In the old graveyard where the shadow clings—
And I had penetrated to the heart of things.

To me their lichened stones were the doorsill
Of some two hundred years of slumber; they
Awaking in me, wakened too the thrill
Of sharing beyond self the infinite play
Of spirit in whatever form it may
Design its being. In outgoing rings
Of clear sensation, wondrously astray,
I was aware of that all weeps or sings,
And I had penetrated to the heart of things.

I was the dune grass in the wind, the quill
That speeds the white gull up the clouded gray;
I was the old man watching, hunched and still,
The swimmer, and the dancers in the hay;
I was the dead who wake but cannot stay,
Whose humble dust has freed them to be kings;
I was the generation on the way,

That, bringing beauty, knows not what it brings,
And I had penetrated to the heart of things.

Prince, there is little more for me to say;
My flight was brief on momentary wings.
Let me remember—only this I pray
Amid life's new rebuffs and buffetings—
That I once penetrated to the heart of things.

On the Boardwalk

MERRY-GO-ROUND, go-round, the sea is saying;
The Boardwalk blooms, the world has gone
        a-Maying.
Merry-go-round, merry-go-round, go-round,
The dragon tramples to the tabor's sound;
The lion, stiff with dignified dismay,
Whirls on behind the horse, his natural prey;
Mild-eyed, the tall giraffe can almost feel
Along her lengthy throat the imagined meal
Crushed from those luscious bulbs of colored light,
That, more than breadfruit, tempt the appetite.
While children mount the fabled steeds and fly
Heavenward beaming. One of them is I.

Not for the ride alone we spend our nickel:
Fortune at times is favorably fickle,
And down the ring-slot suddenly may glide
A shiny brass ring for another ride.
The ocean murmurs, "This I'll not destroy;
Their pompous towers I'll take, but not their toy.
The whirling rhythm vibrates to my own,
Beneath the roar of surf, my undertone,

At whose recurrent, fathomless command,
Foundations of the world are ground to sand.
Merry-go-round, merry-go-round, go-round;
Fly heavenward, children, when the world is
    drowned."

Ah, could the colored lights whirl on forever!
But some mechanic grapples with a lever;
The motion slackens with a sickening jar—
How mercenary these dull people are!
Wait for me, children. Though you may not know it,
I'm deus ex machina and a poet.
Let's break these dirty bills to heaps of change:
We'll scour the jungle and we'll ride the range.
Merry-go-round, merry-go-round, go-round,
The horses prance, the lions wake and bound.
The spring is ours for keeps, and the brass ring
Is ours for keeps, and life, and everything!

The Victim

THE hummingbird that darts and hovers
Made one fatal dart—alas!—
Against a counterfeit of flowers
Reflected in the window glass.
When four-o'clocks had sunk in shadow,
The window caught an extra glint
Of color, like the sudden rainbow
Arching the purple firmament.
Transcendent are the traceries
Illusion weaves to set a snare;
The quick competitor of bees,
Trusting his universe of air

For flight and honey, dazzled so
In quest of sweetness, was waylaid
By something hard that had a glow
Brighter than that the garden made.
Illusion shatters; the ideal
Is much more ruthless than the real.
The visionary hummingbird
Hit nothingness, and hit it hard.

Arcadia

ARCADIA means the Land of Bears,
Not of the Shepherds and their Sheep;
Thus Time, the soft romancer, wears
Away our strength to dreaming sleep,

Gilding the fangs of beasts and rocks
With twilight hazes into grace.
The shepherd's pipe? the mumbling flocks?
I hear the black bear's padded pace.

I, too, have in Arcadia dwelt,
Glossing the name as poets would;
Yet stands, while pastoral dainties melt,
The Bear, where he has always stood.

Over Bright Summer Seas

QUICK! hoist the jib and cast us off, my son,
The racing fleet manoeuvres for the gun,
And we shall stand off shore to give them leeway,—
Eventually they'll crowd us from the seaway.

The handsomest and yet profanest sport
Summons bright argosies from every port,
A dazzling zodiac of racing types,
Stars, Comets, Lightnings, Meteors,—and Snipes,
White on the sunlit blue, and whiter still
Against the shoreline of a shadowed hill,
Mechanical, precise, well disciplined,
Yet, like ourselves, dependent on the wind.

Lord of the wind-torn or the windless sail
To whom Odysseus prayed without avail,
Mad Aeolus!—but how much madder grown
Since weather bureaus claimed you as their own,
The squalls they are too haughty to announce
Swirl east with unpremeditated pounce
And rip the spinnaker's ballooning bubble,
Splinter the heaven-reaching spars to stubble,
Only to add an overdose of balm
And leave all drifting on an oily calm.
Meanwhile, our able sloop pursues her way
Swift without haste, and calm without delay.

Pleased with four knots, incredulous of five,
The cruising sailor does at least arrive,
And somewhere else than where he started from
Breathes deep quiescence of the night to come,
Then hears but echoes underneath the stars
Of disputations in the yacht club bars,
The race re-raced with expletives of wrath
Like flotsam of the tempest's aftermath.
At last no light is showing but his own,
On shore one voice dies out in monotone,
And free from disappointment or success
He slips the mooring of his consciousness.

Hesperides

PAST life and time the island lies
Where once we learned content;
Reflected in far-seeing eyes
That foundered continent:
Green Caspian valley toward the East,
Lost home to the Egyptian priest;
To Athens westward, under far
White Hesperus, Platonic star.

Whichever way the prow is steered
Against the drift of dark,
Darkness itself, so long upreared
Before the wandering barque,
Is on a nimble wind dispersed
Where, had we known it from the first,
The island waits for Hesperus,
For Athens, Egypt, and for us.

Think not my mind, that spurns the fact
And clasps the dream, is swirled
On time's tremendous cataract
Down margins of the world:
In drifts of darkness I affirm
That fact and darkness have their term.
Past death and time the island lies,
And I have seen it with these eyes.

Uneventful Return

It is the time of mooring now;
The pebbles scrape and the reeds are parted
Before the languid push of the prow.

It is the time of mooring now,
And where all day the swallow has darted
Dipping his wings in the sunny waves,
There is only a smooth, dark mirror spread
Where the dancers of the mist will tread.
The air is cool as the breath of caves,
And damp as the breath of steaming loam. . . .

It is the time of mooring now,
Ship your oars and come back home.

Christmas Eve

The snow lies crisp beneath the stars,
    On roofs and on the ground;
Late footsteps crunch along the paths,
    There is no other sound.

So cold it is the roadside trees
    Snap in the rigid frost,
A dreadful night to think on them,—
    The homeless and the lost.

The dead sleep sheltered in the tomb,
    The rich drink in the hall;
The Virgin and the Holy Child
    Lie shivering in a stall.

VARIATIONS ON A THEME

SONNETS

PASTORALS

PROTHALAMION

Variations on a Theme

I

You walk up a deep roadbed to a hilltop;
The trees are splintered and the sun is gray,
Shells rip the cheese-cloth air, and curling gas
That smells of death, out of the lungs of death
Breathes; it is like the sap of slaughtered poplars
Rancid with spring, it is like the breath of old men
Who have been dead a long time but still breathe.
Shell by shell you note the approaching range,
Methodical,—no doubt after a graph
Devised by the professors in Berlin,
And thus defeated by its own precision.
A scattered fire might, by a random chance,
Drape you like garlands on a broken tree,
But this! it is to laugh. You need not wince
Or fling yourself face down in mud until—
Well, until then! By God, they broke the rules;
That nearly got you. You must telegraph
Berlin and file complaints with the professors.
Euclid was wrong. The parallels have met.
But you're all right, stop jabbering the Lord's Prayer,
Since it was answered, and go on with Mozart,
G-minor Symphony, the second movement.
And now with Mozart playing in your skull
Tread daintily among the rats and shell-holes,
Pick your way up the hill between the fragments
Of men and horses, let the blue gas curl.
Listen, the rising voices of the 'cellos,
Lovelier always with the increasing beauty
Of spring, which to an adolescent rapture
Yields not one half its glories, saving all

121

For those whose spring finds winter in their hearts.
These strings are louder, if you listen for them,
Than shells exploding, and dead suns are brighter
Than Verey lights or fear. Death is no rampart
From which, methodical, the fusillades
Of hidden foes come nearer and yet nearer
Until you gauge their range and duck. It is
Not as you think it, not dead breath of poplars;
It is a chance that after sundry warnings
Plotted methodically by distant science,
The shell will miss you, and you will arrive
Up on the hillcrest after lonely walking,
The sun grown splendid for the sunset glory
Hanging above a land ruined but quiet,
And friends whose voices waken you from nightmare,
Singing amid your tangled strands of Mozart:
"The Armistice! We have signed the truce with
    Death!"

II

"What! you were in the war! I'd never guess it
Reading your books. What a strange man you are.
Think of dear Brooke and Seeger and Joyce
    Kilmer,—
Of course, they all met heroes' deaths,—but still
How can experiences so profound
Have failed to leave one comma on your verses?"
"Bird droppings, madam, are not punctuation,
However fair the bird; you do but join
The illimitable clamor of bad causes
That deafen poetry. I must confess
I find not even so faint a trace of verse

As metric crowsfeet in their bloodstained snow.
These causes! You will find ten thousand of them
If you read Gibbon. The damned things are dead.
Search Shakespeare and prepare for me a list
Of his outpourings on the Spanish menace
With rhetoric reserved for the Armada."
"But first, Shakespeare was not aboard that flagship
Of Effingham's; and second, you're not Shakespeare."
"True! True, and thirdly, there is a landscape
Where green Connecticut shrouds Massachusetts
In haze on haze on hills falling away,
Like lovely lies obscuring ugly fact.
I fear—to use geography as figure—
I am Connecticut. I face the ocean,
Yet of its turmoils hear but far-off surf;
I face the mountains yet climb never to them;
I face the mills of booming Massachusetts
Yet do not sweat or jingle coin in pocket;
I face New York and let her lights be distant,
As seasonal shifts on pine and oak
Show the sun changing after winter solstice.
I listen always in my mind to music
That sings away my worries and the world."

III

However much you love your wife, your child,
Time will divide you, and however much
You love yourself, time will divide you also
Into the many pasts you have forgotten.
It is triumphant that the mortal man,
Remembering so many deaths, can still
Sing in the twilight and take heart at dawn

And lift his cup and say: You, my beloved.
Surely beyond that moment's apprehension,
Beyond his conscious thought, beyond the depths
Of his unconscious where the false Messiahs
Bungle amid the delicate corals, and blow
Foul-smelling bubbles to the surface world
And signal with dream-cables: Watch my breath!
Surely beyond thought and all pseudo-science
Of the mind's last profundities, where Faith
Alone is Sea King, surely the soul dwells,
Timeless, immortal, alert to songs of earth
And knowing that when he says: You, my beloved,
Echoes start out and ring the golden spheres
To meet in perfect circles beyond space
And there to find again the voice they sprang from.
This is good physics, you who disbelieve
Acknowledge that your voice has also started
Motion throughout the Universe, and never
Though you should chase it through Paolo's
        whirlwind
Shall you catch up with it. You'd eat your words
But can not, while throughout resounding space
The syllables of love clap laughing hands.
Whatever starts in time can not be stopped.
Wherefore lift up your hearts all you that love
Gravely as well as passionately; wherefore
Take heed, you wastrels of the sacred word.
For time bequeaths her patience to eternity
Wherein so many ages beyond counting
Have poured what seemed immense and what was
        lost
In immensity and found in new dimensions.
However much you love your wife, your child,
Time will divide you, and beyond division
Eternity echoes: "You, you my beloved."

IV

The dead are not dead. Look, they are the living,
We see them in the dance of atoms, sunlight
Dazzles their garments all too swift in passing!
How set the mouth within the stiffened grave,
How closed the eyes:—and have you ever seen
Discarded day-clothes mimicking the dancer?
Fair spring, how shall we learn to greet you now
Cased in this double cloth of heart and mind!
But later, surely—do I rightly guess?—
With echo of these unextinguishable
Violins we shall climb beyond the sunlight
Into the sun itself, and there take on
Bright immortality, ourselves the spring.
Angry or gay a while, we do forget
That the gray body, bleak though unresisting
To death its paramour, was once a child
Slender and elegant diving into the sea.
O triumph of delight beyond the world!
Now for this moment we are sure, we know
The calm that through our long vicissitudes
Has sung of triumph to the splendid end.
This green and pleasant land where sings the
          woodthrush
And all day long soft wind in sunlit leaves,
Remembers Babylon, and looks on Moscow
Where a Lenin à Becket lies in state for pilgrims,
Merely as one more in the list of causes
Man makes to vent his passion against death.
Death was the Tarquin king who raped Lucrece,
Death the last emperor of Byzantium,
Death was disguised as Marie Antoinette,
Death the five murdered kings of England, Death
The Czar of all the Russias,—so they think

And like the roysterers in Chaucer's tale,
They set out hotfoot to dismember Death
And fall to quarreling among themselves
And slay each other. No new worlds come forth
From folly so short-sighted. Let us know
The only active war or revolution
Each man must fight within his soul, when God
Permits a gray sun over smoky fields
To blur the outward light and inward music.
Clear melody can make men forget fear,
Clear sunlight seizes on the words of lovers
And vibrates through all space and beyond space.
This quiet afternoon, itself eternal,
Rings with a thousand echoes, and love's voices
Speak out, and at the hillcrest there is peace.

SONNETS

1. Repartee

As ONE who bears beneath his neighbor's roof
Some thrust that staggers his unready wit,
And brooding through the night on such reproof
Too late conceives the apt reply to it;
So all our life is but an afterthought,
A puzzle solved long past the time of need,
And tardy wisdom that one failure bought
Finds no occasion to be used in deed.
Fate harries us; we answer not a word,
Or answering too late, we waste our breath;
Not even a belated quip is heard
From those who bore the final taunt of death;
And thus the Jester parries all retort:
His jest eternal, and our lives so short.

II. The Wild Philosopher

THE wild philosopher surveyed the scenes
Where rubble of humanity's best thought
Lay in the after-fumes of gaunt machines,
Decided the whole case was hopeless, sought
Comfort in his wine cellar, that cool cave,
And taking sundry bottles from the shelf,
Quoted Li Po: "Seeing all men behave
Like drunkards, why stay sober by myself?"
As he refilled his glass from time to time
Snatches of music, memories of youth
Came back to him, and suddenly sublime
With purpose as a man half crazed by truth,
He sprang up brandishing a new idea—
Nay, more than that, the Cosmic Panacea!

III. More

ALWAYS more riches, more enjoyment, more
Of everything the world can briefly give,
Though through your avid hands as through a sieve
Beauties unnumbered and unnoticed pour.
You chase the wind, but you are fugitive
From the great quiet at the whirlwind's core,
And spendthrift of life's measurable store
You have not purchased the mere right to live.
There is a vacant seat beside me here
Where you may rest and watch the season change;
Form, color, tone, mysterious or clear,
In swift variety though never strange,
Where if one beauty wholly be revealed
Life will have yielded all she has to yield.

iv. Platitude

DULL platitude, worn coin from wisdom's mint,
You purchase still your phrase's worth of truth
While clever counterfeits for all their glint
Buy but the penny sophistries of youth.
Lacklustre, thin, the date illegible,
Scarred by the teeth of every sceptic age,
Your metal still rings true as when it fell
New-minted from the furnace of a sage.
The novelty of noon is out of date
By night; the timeless gold, however worn,
In undiminished worth will circulate
From hands long dust to others yet unborn.
Let counterfeiters buy the world! The wise
Save thriftily for larger merchandise.

v. By Many Paths

BY MANY paths we reach the single goal,
And all our quarrels deal but with its name;
There is no soul so different from my soul
As in its essence to be not the same.
No warrior but in his heart must know
How triumph is not proud nor vengeance sweet,
For he beholds, who slays the kindred foe,
Himself, self-murdered, lying at his feet.
It has been written that we are the islands
Which, ocean-sundered into seeming twain,
Are truly of one continent, the highlands
Wrought of one rock and rooted in one plain.
Bright Himalayan peace! the humblest crest
One with the splendor of Mount Everest.

VI. The Wind Is from the North

AND now at sunset, ripples flecked with gold
Leap lightly over the profounder blue;
The wind is from the north, and days are few
That still divide us from the winter cold.
O, it was easy when the dawn was new
To make the vow that never should be old,
But now at dusk the words are not so bold,—
Thus have I learned. How fares the hour with you?
A heron rises from the trembling sedge,
His vigil at an end. Mine too is done.
A late sail twinkles on the watery edge,
And up the shore lights sparkle one by one.
Seasons will change before tomorrow's sun,
So speaks the dune-grass on the windy ledge.

VII. The Wind Is from the South

SOME of that August day's long dead delight
Came back to me, as on a winter hill
I saw red sunset fall away, and spill
Its scattered embers on the hearth of night.
We two had always been so calm, so still,
That silence was not lonely, and in spite
Of shadow deepening over snowy white,
A warmth, as of your presence, smote the chill.
Whatever men may call the real, the true,
This much I know indeed, that an immense
And actual radiance such as only you
Have ever given to my mortal sense
Gleamed on the hillside and then vanished hence;
And all that winter night the south wind blew.

VIII. The Letter

LAST night I wrote a letter to my friend:
I said, "Come back, the years are getting cold,
And, as our lives wear on and we grow old,
Loneliness will be frightening toward the end."
I called you back, but you shall not behold
Impulsive phrases that Desire has penned;
Last night I wrote what I shall never send,
The pages your white hands shall not unfold.
Pride locked my desk and threw the key away,
For Pride is less impulsive than Desire;
Perhaps a stranger, finding it some day,
Will yield the faded secret to the fire,
Where it will join in dust those separate dead,
Sorrow, who wrote, and Love, who never read.

IX. He Who in Spring's Rebirth Has Put His Trust

HE WHO in spring's rebirth has put his trust
Now answers not to April or to May,
Nor sees the moon-white apple blossom sway,
Nor breathes its sweetness on the evening gust.
He who was first to climb the height of day
Lies full-length in the valley of the dust;
His sword sleeps in his hand, and it is rust;
His heart sleeps in his breast, and it is clay.
Brother, so mute among the fallen years,
We come at dayspring to your living tomb
That is the green earth, and we shed no tears,
Knowing that if you wait for us elsewhere

Soon will you give us loving welcome there,
And if you perished, then we share your doom.

x. Requiem

THIS high, thin tone that from the violin
Spins to the lark its thread-like note until
Spilling a rainbow on the cloud far in
The west it trembles and is scattered, will
With such high delicacy likewise sing
Lingering grief to a celestial end
Splendid in death, as though an earthly thing
Extinguished in bright music should ascend,
Ascend, and to the earthly heart be lost,
That now released from grief can beat again,
Having once wrought at so complete a cost
High beauty from deep sorrow not in vain.
So weeping ends. So music ends. The whole
Transfigured world welcomes the homing soul.

xi. Overheard

THE windswept beach was empty but for three
Who paced the foamline of the rising tide.
The two, mother and son, looked out to sea,
The third, invisible, walked at their side.
He shouted to them. (Hear the salt wind sighing.)
He wrung his hands. (The air is growing chill.)
He cried aloud, "You see the gray gull flying,
Can't you see me, Matilda? Can't you, Bill?"
A sudden notion swept into her head:
"You look more like your father all the time."
"I don't! I look just like myself," he said,
And then both smiled like partners in a crime.

The third was writhen into wisps of pain
And scattered into the gray fog again.

XII. The Termites

BLIND to all reasoned aim, this furtive folk
Breed to destroy, destroy to breed once more,
As they go gnawing tunnels in the floor
That turn to yellow dust as fine as smoke.
Sometimes a hushing slide within the core
Of beams gave warning where some fiber broke,
And someone said, "This house is solid oak:
No fear, it's stood two centuries and more."
And still the midnight work advanced, and still
The sleepers in their forebears' house slept on,
Till the house sank and vanished; roof to sill,
It fell to dust—all but the termites gone;
And these devoured each other or took flight
To scatter more destruction through the night.

XIII. Thermopylae

MEN lied to them and so they went to die.
Some fell, unknowing that they were deceived,
And some escaped, and bitterly bereaved,
Beheld the truth they loved shrink to a lie.
And those there were that never had believed,
But from afar had read the gathering sky,
And darkly wrapt in that dread prophecy,
Died hoping that their truth might be retrieved.
It matters not. For life deals thus with Man;
To die alone deceived or with the mass,
Or disillusioned to complete his span.

Thermopylae or Golgotha, all one,
The young dead legions in the narrow pass;
The stark black cross against the setting sun.

In Time of Mistrust *

I

THIS is no idle rhetoric to reach
Your ears for this occasion, though I use
Some figures that are common to our speech,
Some noble words made weak with long abuse.
For I have seen winds blow the forest down,
And I have seen some sturdy trees survive;
Death have I seen, and war, and I have known
The miracles that keep the soul alive.
And I have known, as well, the Things that kill
With a long death those unsubstantial men
Who would with money or with systems fill
The human void, that shall be void until
The spirit is acknowledged once again
As lord of Things. We shall be richer, then.

II

It was the morning after the great wind
Had wrecked my country, and the twentieth year

* These are eight of the original fourteen sonnets that composed
the Phi Beta Kappa Poem at the College of William and Mary
in 1939. They were written in the months between the great
hurricane of 1938 and the outbreak of World War II, and were
dedicated to my friend, the late John Stewart Bryan, then president of William and Mary.

Since I had heard more mad destruction dinned
Through war-torn woods of this distracted sphere.
Yet in the trampled wreckage of the wood
Ripped by the wind from its New England earth,
A red tree and a yellow tree withstood,
In forthright autumn promise of rebirth.
And in this shattered forest which I thought
Destroyed beyond the hope of future springs,
The lonely guard against oblivion wrought
Its dream of new leaves and returning wings.
As in a shattered world, the lonely few
From the old wisdom must create the new.

III

The Good remains for ever undefined,
But we have known through all our wanderings:
First, that true pleasure must be of the mind;
Second, that no man can be slave to Things.
We cannot conquer spiritual evil
When we are lost in Things of speed and sense;
Our love of Things, our hatred of the Devil,
Cancel in one supine indifference.
The arsenal of peace is down already
When peace itself is torn by inner war:
The enemies are one at heart and steady,
In dedication, far superior:
Evil they may be, but at least they know
That passive Good is a self-conquered foe.

IV

Evil may also have its mystic vision,—
Bright Lucifer himself was Star of Morning,—

Immune to pity or the world's derision
It triumphs after a contemptuous warning.
The mightiest sinner like the mightiest saint
Must rend his spirit to achieve his goal,
Ascetic to mere crime or fleshly taint
He wins complete perversion of the soul.
Magnificently Evil thunders on,
Finding no Holiness to match its wrath;
All values are reversed, all boundaries gone,
The entire world becomes its open path.
Evil has spirit, though with downward wings,
While Good lies torpid, paralyzed by Things.

V

Some would attack, however much they fear it,
The outward form of the monstrosity;
To us the darker war against that spirit
Without whose power the monster could not be.
Never by fury, firing shot for shot,
Can the Good triumph, brother killing brother,
Ages of history attest it, but
We still supplant one evil with another.
To us the darker war, to us the dive
Like the old hero's to the monster's den,
Where earthly weapons fail, and we must strive
In darkness with those lights vouchsafed to men:
The minds that meditate, the souls that summon
To human help the Power that made us human.

VI

The search itself is the fulfilment; now
When we are nagged by every sterile cause,

Let us renew, amid these brawls, our vow
Of contemplation to the ancient laws.
In groves where no wind reaches to destroy,
Where Time itself dies with the sunset wind,
Let us renew our spiritual joy,
The boundless freedom of the disciplined.
We shall be jeered at, as the uncouth host
Jeered at the patience of that monkish toil
Whose beacons marked upon a windswept coast
Where wisdom had found refuge from turmoil,—
The flight beyond the world for those who must
Preserve some pattern for the whirling dust.

VII

Light of this world, whom the world tries to darken,
Lord of this world, whom faith alone can find,
Word of this world, to whom men will not hearken,
Bright presence to whose radiance men are blind,
View with compassion your revolving wheel,
That primal gift, now whirling to destruction;
Your gold converted to a blast of steel,
Your wisdom twisted by adroit corruption.
In lonely spirits here and there inflame
Austere enthusiasm for the plan
When in your image first, and then your name,
Would have created the triumphant Man.
Speak immortality through them, wage war
On Things men worship, that men live once more.

VIII

That men may live, and on the morning hills
The sun may rise not only to reveal

The ruin, but as well the sentinels
Who guard our future good from present ill.
Then shall we, like glad wakers from despair,
Throw off the dark dream, and once more accept
Our interval of earth and sun and air
Even in forests where the mad wind swept.
It will be such a day as all redeemers
Have died for, though they seemed to die in vain.
The evil men of violence, the schemers
Who whispered violence to helpless dreamers,
Shall with their dark dream die. And wakened men,
With God, once wakened, will not sleep again.

Pastorals

I

So GHOSTLY then the girl came in
I never saw the turnstile twist
Down where the orchard trees begin
Lost in a revery of mist.

And in the windless hour between
The last of daylight and the night,
When fields give up their ebbing green
And two bats interweave their flight,

I saw the turnstile glimmer pale
Just where the orchard trees begin,
But watching was of no avail,
Invisibly the girl came in.

I took one deep breath of the air
And lifted up my heavy heart;

It was not I who trembled there
But my immortal counterpart.

I knew that she had come again
Up from the orchard through the stile,
Without a sign to tell me when,
Though I was watching all the while.

II

So soft in the hemlock wood
The phoenix sang his lullaby,
Shepherds drowsed where they stood,
Slumber felled each passerby,
And lovers at their first caress
Slept in virgin loneliness.

Not for mortal eye to see
Naked life arise from embers;
Only the dark hemlock tree,
Evergreen itself, remembers
How the Word came into being,
No man hearing, no man seeing.

From the taut bow of sleep
Shoots the phoenix toward the day,
Shepherds wake and call their sheep,
Wanderers go on their way.
Unaware how death went by,
Lovers under the hemlocks lie.

III

The fireflies wink and glow,
The night is on the march,

The cricket clacks his castanets
And the moon hangs in the larch.
I will take my violin
And a few themes I will play:
Pizzicati for the fireflies,
Harmonics for the moonlight,
And a chord for the smell of hay.

I will play but a few bars,
And when the moon has set
I will listen to the stars.

IV

Blessëd be the spring
From the moss-green rock,
Where if no nymph sing
To shepherd and his flock,
Still music flows
Lovely as the search
Of water toward the sea
Where flowing waters end.
Time blows down
The oak tree and birch,
Time will be
A foe and then a friend.
The little spring is clear,
The little spring is cold,
And though this year
My heart feels old,
The spring flows on
As when the grove stood
Before gray time
Blew down the wood.

It still sings on
Where nymphs and shepherds pass
In time long gone,
In time that never was.

V

The wise old apple tree in spring,
Though split and hollow, makes a crown
Of such fantastic blossoming
We cannot let them cut it down.
It bears no fruit, but honey bees
Prefer it to the other trees.

The orchard man chalks his mark
And says, "This empty shell must go."
We nod and rub it off the bark
As soon as he goes down the row.
Each spring he looks bewildered. "Queer,
I thought I marked this thing last year."

Ten orchard men have come and gone
Since first I saw my grandfather
Slyly erase it. I'm the one
To do it now. As I defer
The showy veteran's removal
My grandson nods his full approval.

Like mine, my fellow ancient's roots
Are deep in the last century
From which our memories send shoots
For all our grandchildren to see
How spring, inviting bloom and rhyme,
Defeats the orchard men of time.

VI

Piping Anne and husky Paul
Once they swelled our madrigal,
She watched him and he watched her,
Always out of tune they were.
Yet from two discords may be
Love's most tuneful harmony;
Such a music they have wrought,
              (they have wrought)
As to set our skill at naught.

Let the nightingale in vain
Lift his amorous refrain,
Let the dying reedy swan
Cease her prothalamion.
They are sunk in such a bliss
Deep as old Atlantic is.
End our song and come away
              (come away)
Music hath no more to say.

VII

"Here I am, though you're past caring,"
  Sang the bird on the bough,
"Daft in the dawn, despairing,
  With cold dew on your brow,
  Afraid she has failed you now.
    I'll sing her a welcome—hark,
      Such notes as never were heard,
      And she'll say, 'What is that bird?
    No thrush or meadowlark.
No nightingale or dove,
  No phoenix flaming by,

Or a swan winging to die—
It must be the bird of love!'

"She's coming, although you gave up hoping,"
   Sang the bird from the tree,
"And you'd have gone off moping
   To hang yourself maybe
   If it had not been for me.
     Beauty the day adorning,
       More than the heart can hold,
       She moves through a maze of gold,
     Dear mistress of the morning.
Go to her, run, young lover,
   Although your running seem
   Cumbered as in a dream,
Go, for my song is over!"

VIII

Now on the idle pond
Slowly the fallen leaf
Drifts with its double.

Crescent from prow to poop,
Curving with curves of gold,
Galley of silence.

How have our pomps decayed!
Frail is the royal barge,
Autumn the cargo.

IX

Is it the aster, silvered in the dark;
Or leaf-smoke, or the silence of the frost,

Or, from beyond the valleys I have crossed,
The thin defiance of the fox's bark,—

Is it these Autumn signs of change and night
Which slowly drain my arteries of time,
Until I lose myself, my breath, my sight,
One with the drifting smoke and silvering rime?

Ebbing with them toward Winter, knowing
    only,
One fading moment: how I closed the door
Of home behind me; then, not even lonely,
At last forgot I could return no more.

X

The grapes are ripe, the frost is near,
The cricket sounds a rusty note,
And the bluebird at the close of year
Repeats the April song by rote.

Day still is warm, but after dark
Autumn advances leaf by leaf;
And the watchdog with a nervous bark
Halts an imaginary thief.

XI

In solemn pause the forest waits
The signal to return;
Within our rotting garden gates
The weeds of autumn burn.

Father to son we held our field
Against the siege of tares,
Knowing our weaker sons would yield
The land no longer theirs.

Knowing how wind and sun and rain
Would fling their green stampedes
Where we who harvested the grain
Lie buried under weeds.

XII

Shutters bang in the wind outside;
Cobwebs hang from the mildewed walls;
Stale, damp mould in the lifeless cold;
Doors flung wide to the darkened halls.

Love and strength of the new, keen race
Lie full length where the weeds grow high,
All things swept to the past except
This ruined place the wind roars by.

Blank disaster of empty windows;
Broken plaster strewn on the floor;
Darkness spills from the wild, bleak hills,
And the winter wind blows under the door.

XIII

The moon is aloft,
The wind lies still,
Voices come soft
From Hickory Hill.

But there's nobody there
To whisper a word,
No one to hear
Or be overheard.

I only remember
The moon all white
On the clear November
Hill at night.
But the words we left
That other year
Surely drift
From the hillside there.

And no one would dare
Clear nights in the fall
To stand listening there—
I least of all.

XIV

Hunched at angles
Over new snow
The ironwood tree.
Crotch of bough
Tufted with snow
And nothing to see
Of leaf and of leaf
That a few weeks ago
Were the ironwood tree.
Skeleton now
It is bole and bough,
A perch for a crow
Or a chickadee

With feathers ruffed back
When the winds blow.
And below
There is only new snow
And nothing to see
Or leaf and of leaf
Or of you,
Or of me.

XV

Let us for ever be at peace
As walls and mountains are,
Or as the ocean storms that cease
When smoother tides would hold a star.
We strove with shadows for so long,
We sped our youth so fast.
But now the bell has rung for evensong
And sleep, at last.

How many frolics we have seen
Who now shall frisk no more,
And made pretense of budding green
When autumn ripened at the core.
When wit was wanting words were long
And folly made reply,
Now all our words are but good-night, our song
A lullaby.

XVI

Had you but time
For a brief survival,

A single rhyme
Before Death's arrival,
What would you say?
What would you sing?
Before close of day
And of everything.

You'd say, "I have seen
The rose leaf fall
On shadowed, green
Grass by the wall."
You'd sing, "If it stayed
Its beauty would cloy,
That was meant and was made
For one morning's joy."

Prothalamion

I

LAMP of the West, held high aloft
By hand unseen of her whose name
Thou bearest; star when nights are soft
And earth breathes skyward the faint flame
Of pungent green wherein is mingled
Wild cherry's virginal, keen smell;
White Venus, singled
From galaxies to be the guide
Of man and bride,
Take thou our thanks for this thy miracle.

The silver-footed girl once crept
And leaned far out the window ledge
To ponder when they thought she slept,
Thy twin lights at the water's edge;

Until as sparks among the embers
Die, thine image waned away,
But she remembers,
And for the wonder thou hast wrought
A votive thought
She offered on the threshold of the Day.

Yet spring was late this year; the snow
Still hid thee and the garden paled
Beneath a withered moon, as though
For once thy miracle had failed.
Thin oak leaves, ghosts of foliage, clung
Above the new year in the sheath,
And where they hung
Cold shadow hid the snow from day
So that it lay
Round every tree-trunk like a faded wreath.

Now comes thine hour. This marriage eve
Will I alone thy vigil keep,
While maiden-fingered fancies weave
For her upon the loom of sleep
Pictures of the inviolate land
More beautiful than snow, where she
Needs not my hand
To guide her, where she reigns in light
One last, long night,
Untrammeled by our fair conspiracy.

While I, leaning against the wicket,
Watch thy reflection in the pond,
And feel a rhythm through grass and thicket—
My pulse of life, swelling beyond
My veins, beating through space and far
Away where even thy glories blur,

O chosen star!
Yet she eludes us still this hour;
A chaster power
Than ours fills all the universe with her.

But thou and I shall call her back.
Love swoons in those vast periods;
Her feet stray in the heaving black
So far from the more homely gods.
O call her as she comes to me
Tomorrow in the lovers' dawn,
Clean as the sea,
Her gainly body tense with a surmise
That veils her eyes,
Not furtive but most regally withdrawn.

Behind her morning overarches,
Tiers of crimson fire that make
Greener the violent green of larches,
Bluer the calm blue of the lake.
The white swan drifts in mirrored sleep,
The haze is tangled in the rushes;
Clear and deep
A drop of dew rings in the pond
And fields respond
With songs of robins, meadowlarks, and thrushes.

Now, Love, I call thee, and am heard
By none but thee, I speak thy name;
I wed thee with a secret word
In accent quiet as a flame.
I say thou art the one who arrives
For ever, who never shall depart;
Through a thousand lives
When fields are sweetened beneath the sun

Thou art the one
Who wakes the immortal in the mortal heart.

Hasten! we have not long against
That hour of pomp when we must see
Our rocky garden neatly fenced,
Our love in mild captivity.
Now dawn spreads open like a fan
Of sultry fire, the wet leaves stir;
Girl and man
Pass through the elemental gate,
For spring was late
And now the summer has caught up with her.

At the waterside a tree is growing
Whose blossoms crowd the drifting air,
And of its fruit there is no knowing
Till thou hast tasted of it there.
Its dark leaves in the morning chime
Not of the morning or the night,
But of the time
Between the chaos and the flame
When softly came
The Word that made eternal love's delight.

Eternal the brief joy of flesh,
The finite infinite and whole,
The thwarted body fired afresh
By flames that mount into the soul.
The fruit shall follow the tree-in-flower
With ripe fulfilment after pain;
This is the hour,
The golden rift in time wherefrom
Surely shall come
The song of love-in-death made life again.

But thou, so young; more meet for thee
The birches tossing their green hair!
What blossom crowns the darker tree—
Joy? But thy pain I can not share.
This night I yield thee back to sleep,
This night, the last of loneliness,
I fold thee deep
In peace and ask no more until
Dawn floods the hill,
Not even thy phantom-self for a caress.

And now the curved horizon covers
Love's star that melts away in light.
Lamp of the West, fail not thy lovers
When after another day, the night
Shall lift thee in its arms, and I
In mine shall hold thy counterpart,
Thou in thy sky
And we in ours, until we rest
Beyond the west
Where death lies slain beneath the single heart.

II

The hills turn hugely in their sleep
With sound of grinding rock and soil
While down their granite shoulders leap
The waterbrooks in white turmoil.
The vigil of Good Friday done,
Our second spring ascends the height;
The earth turns southward toward the sun,
And trees which guard the pascal door,
In leaf once more,
Once more are murmurous with strange delight.

For now is the world's Eastertide,
And born that they may die again
Arise from death the gods who died.
Osiris, slender as young grain,
Comes back to Isis; the shy lad
Adonis wakens by the stream;
And Jesus, innocently clad
In samite, walks beneath the trees,
Half ill-at-ease
That Judas and the Cross were but a dream.

And thou art she whom I have seen
Always, but never understood,
In broken shrines festooned with green,
In twilight chapels of the wood;
Or on the hills a shepherdess
Walked with the sun full on her face,
And though her body and her dress
Apparelled her in meek disguise,
I dropped my eyes,
For still I knew the goddess by her pace.

I know thee now in morning light
Though thou are wrought of flesh and blood,
And though the mother of the night
Resumes at dawn her maidenhood;
And though love severed with his knife
The girdle of the million years
And yielded to importunate life
The toll she asks of those who still
Would journey, till
They pass her known and visible frontiers.

The children from beyond the sun
Come bounding down the hillside grass,

And in the joyous rout is one
Who smiles and will not let us pass.
He stands, the fairest of them all,
And in his loveliness I trace
Thy loveliness. His light footfall
Bends not the grass he treads upon;
But he is gone
Before my eyes have feasted on his face.

In undulant desire we merge,
On tides of light we sport and rest;
We swerve up from the deeper surge
To hover on the trembling crest
Of joy, and when the wave has passed,
Then smooth is the swing to the abyss
Of quietness, where with a last
Eye-darkening smile, we say farewell
Until the spell
Shall be renewed. Forget all things but this.

No grass-blade bends, no shadow stirs;
Love mounted high, slumber is deep;
Deep is the spring beneath the firs,
A sweet and lonely place for sleep.
And waking, we shall cool our flesh
In depths so clear they seem as air;
Twofold in beauty, thou refresh
Thy body in that water, bright
With muted light,
And brighter still for thy reflection there.

While I along the bank shall find
The flowers that opened with the day
Still dew-drenched, and with these entwined
New fronds of fern or darker bay.

Or pausing in a shaft of sun
That strikes across the mottled glade
Watch thee too long, beloved one,
Watch thee with eyes grown big with tears
Because the years
Suddenly spoke and made my heart afraid.

We must not to a foe like time
Yield up our present. Take my hand
And up the morning we shall climb
Until the wooded valley land
Lies all beneath us in the drowse
Of love's meridial aftermath;
The trellis of entwining boughs
Trembles in the great joy of green,
But does not screen
The comfortable glimpse of homeward path.

We will not to our ancient foe
Yield up this happiness; it lies
Shielded from sickle and from snow
And all the menace of the skies.
At night I shall watch over thee,
The future safe beneath thy breast,
And after autumn there shall be
Dayspring, when for each other's sake
We shall awake
And follow Love beyond the unknown west.

THE GATES
OF THE COMPASS

THE GATES OF THE COMPASS

1. Memory

THE huntsman riding through the fogs of dawn
Lifts to his lips the horn of twisted gold
And blows two bell-like notes through glen and hollow
Mournfully keen as smoke of autumn leaves.
For ever young he rides a dying horse,
For ever on the chase though no stag flies,
Attended only by those double echoes
The soul and flesh, the day and night of time.
Until the blindfold of the fog between
His eyes and the far reaches of the day
Grows thin, and all around him he beholds
A countryside bathed in the light of dream.
And there dismounting, he goes forth alone
And blows the single golden note of peace.

If from all memories you ravelled one
Down the dark labyrinth of mind, what doors
Would open and what vistas be revealed
Among the many pasts you have forgotten?
I ask you of your birthplace, and you tell
Of leafy streets, a frame house on a terrace,
An apple tree with boughs that touched the ground
And made a cave of cider-smelling earth.
But dive beneath your thoughts. There you remember
The new-flung planet flaming into space
When it gave birth to something kin to you
In the dim dawn of life. Dive farther yet
And you will find perhaps like a deep pearl

Sunk under leagues of troubled sea, your Self.
If from all memories you ravelled one
You could return behind time's double rhythm
And casting off the blindfold walls of space
Look clearly on what now is mystery.
But memory is frail and tenuous,
An evening cobweb drifting on the air
That weaves a rainbow down its wavering length,
Divides, entangles other strands, till soon
You are enmeshed in clinging gossamers
So subtle that to bind one to a thought
Were to destroy the airy fantasy.

Two bells that ring through fog,—what sorrow moves
Uneasily behind the curtained years?
Follow that memory until you see
A small boy grimy with the July heat
Sitting disconsolate upon the steps,
His eyes full, his chin cupped in his hands;
O many years ago, and yet you find
Your heart not uncompassionate of his.
The air was milky with the powder smoke
From firecrackers. All the afternoon
Two slow bells, tuned a minor third apart,
Clang after clang rang out the solemn news:
The Spanish fleet is sunk, the Spanish fleet
Is sunk at Santiago. . . . The Spanish fleet,
The Spanish fleet is sunk at Santiago.
The tears stung through the grime upon your cheeks
And you were dully sure that through all time
This sorrow would not fade. Those were your ships
That had been sunk, you loved their sounding names
And all their strangeness; they were proud and golden
Armadas on the oceans of your fancy,
Freighted with the imaginings of days,

Each day a lifetime; now they were yours no longer.
The elegant *Vizcaya,* curved and gilded,
The slim *Teresa,* her long masts aslant,
The *Almirante Oquendo,* high of prow,
The *Cristobal Colon,* her funnels set
Rakishly fore and aft the single mast,
And the destroyers, *Pluton* and *Furor,*
The pitiful, the vincible armada,
Scarce worth the Sunday morning's target practice.
You knew them all from keel to fighting-tops,
And saw the dawn-red waters of the harbor
As one by one against the shoreline hills
The doomed ships poured to gain the open sea.
The flames leapt from their funnels as they flew
And the foam fountained in a double jet
Before their prows; but speed, desperate speed
Was quite in vain. The grey ships hemmed them in.
The first gun boomed, a hundred others answered,
And the air whined and flickered with the shells.
As the first courser in a cavalry charge
Struck by a bullet jumps into the air
And stumbles to his death, the stricken ships
Reared to the sheet of flame, wallowed, and swung
In aimless curves, then brandishing their masts
Against the sky, cast up their gilded sterns
And burst with dull explosions undersea.
The two bells of that shabby triumph clang,
Still clang, the bells of victory still clang,
Unto this day time booms upon two bells
With drift of drizzling echoes in the mist,
For when your Spanish ships went down, you learned
That by whatever names they may be called,
Things beautiful and happy are foredoomed.
Your childish heart held more than childish woe
Not to be comforted till you should see

The Spanish fleet come sailing home from limbo,
And even fancy could not blur the knowledge
That they would never come, and that was ended.
There was a horror in the victory,
Something eternal left you at that moment
Confirmed apprentice to your master, Time.

Seize on another strand of memory
And follow. You were playing blind man's buff
With other children in a darkening room.
The bandage pressed so tight upon your eyes
That stars and flashes flickered to and fro.
You were bewildered as your playmates changed
To savage ambushes of touch and sound,
Brushing against you, pinching, plucking at you,
And muttering in far corners of the room.
You heard soft footsteps going away, and then
Nothing but silence. Were they gone? or hiding?
You waited a long while, grew slowly frightened,
Then cold with panic snatched the blindfold off
And stared into the void of a black room.
You were alone. Through the two open windows
Where the blue twilight glimmered, two bells
          clanged.
You whispered, "I must run into the hall."
Then with a voice that scarcely could be heard:
"Is anybody here?" "Of course, of course,
Turn up the gas. Darling, it's only a game;
Look, here's your rabbit. Here is Doctor Bun.
Now Doctor Bun, tell him it was a game;
They didn't mean it; everything's all right."
And so your patent of mortality
Was sealed, both by the double note of time
And the dark walls of space, which hedged you in
Henceforth from the wide reaches of the day.

You tell me you were born . . . where was it then?
I have forgotten. Follow deeper still
To a world blind with steam through which the sun
Glimmers uncertainly with bloodshot light.
There you stand in ooze up to your ankles,
And all around except for where the sea
Whimpers along the edges of the marsh
The jungle closes in with drip of leaves
And gurgle of hot mud where bubbles swell
With vapor, puff, collapse, and swell again.
A scaly head comes bulging through the muck
And stares with witless and unwinking eyes.
Then the ground heaves, a tremor quivers through it,
The fog sighs palely with a lightning flash,
Low thunder booms, and from the middle sky
The echo travels back in minor thirds.
There in that shadowless expanse you stand
While something horrible you can not name
Gathers along your spine. The fog thickens
And then the horror is upon you. Night.

O well to live above these memories,
Well for your reason in his upper sky
To shine through the clear air of fact, nor pierce
Too deep into the fog of nether worlds.
O well for you . . . but think not to forget
The savage birthplace I remember for you.
Look at the pliant skin which clothes your hands,—
Look closer. Ah, the lizard scales, the pores
Agape to breathe the hot steam of the marsh.
The jungle seethes, and lust with roving eyes
That shine through darkness, leaps upon despair
And mates with her. And when the wandering moon
Half-seen through never-lifting depth of fog
Has nine times closed her circle in the dawn

Despair brings forth the wonder-child of lust.
These were your parents in that early birthplace
And in the lowest marches of your mind
They prowl the jungle of the double thunder
Screaming against the filtered light of reason
As dogs behowl the moon, till reason's self,
Faint with the fumes from those primeval fens,
Swoons in the zenith. O desperate one,
Will you return to that dank world you left
Æons ago, or plunging boldly through it
Traverse yet farther to that other day
Which lies beyond it, where the unbroken light
Before the worlds were, brought you into being?
If in the short progression of this earth
You have thrown wide the doors of life and seen
The jungle creatures, shrunk to tiny vermin,
Scatter from sight among the mouldy walls,
And the vast trees, diminishing through ages,
Become the fronds of horsetail and of fern
You trample down on paths of afternoon,
You shall yet see all things that knew the jungle
Shrink, while the spirit grows till it behold
This burnt-out planet smaller than an ember
Whirling from sight along an autumn wind.

At dawn when you awake from your short sleep
And the poor dream of living that you had,
You shall arise and wash your heart with laughter
Under the trees beside the shadowed waters.
Come, snatch the blindfold off, and hush the bells
That ring against the Spanish fleets of dream,
Behold around the final headland steaming,
Vizcaya, Cristobal Colon, Oquendo,
Teresa, Pluton, Furor,—homeward bound.

II. The Nightmare

WE COME on leaden feet, we come with leaden
Tread along the haunted corridors
Through darkness void as in a dying brain
Where one by one the thoughts have flickered out.
The curves of our grey surplices flow soft
In every crevice of your memory,
And not an ingle of your mind or body
Eludes our still invasion. You shall hear
The fields whispering under the thin rain
Raw on autumnal earth though spring is here.
We will wring acid tears that bite the eyes
For someone dead whom you have never seen.
Hear how unending rain upon his grave
Seeps downward till it whimpers on his bones.
He loved the glow of fire upon his hands
That now lie splashed with mud beneath the rain,—
Think of him out there when you wake at midnight.

You never knew him, but we tell you, we
Whose office is to enlist the death-watch for him,
In him you weep the doom that is your own.
Look at your hands, the blue veins showing through,
Fantastically outlined against the fire.
The rain will sog the fingers like the petals
Which lie on the wet grass when spring is done.

You will remember Love, cry out to Love,
Who held your body close against the world;
You will remember how the arms of Love
Were round you in the little curtained room
Where the clock ticked. You will remember how
With every slash of rain against the window
When the wind wailed, she drew you ever closer

And pressed you down, so safe, so kind she was
And joyful in the secret gifts of love.
You will call out to her from underground
As children from their nightmares call for help:
Beloved, look! My body is so cold.
The earth seeps in on me and the cold rain;
Fling back the curtain, tell me this is a dream,
Wake me! deliver me! I am gagged with death.
She will not hear you, she will never come.

You did not know the dead man, so you say.
But you have known those who have followed him.
Think of them out there. What? so soon forgotten?
And of what merits, then, are you possessed
To ensure a longer dwelling in remembrance?
Think of each one in turn. Give them your name,
Think how they held their hands out to the fire
And glowed through every vein. They saw no end
To the anatomy of thought and sinew
Which made their universe,—themselves the universe;
They were important beings to themselves.

Count over all your friends, your loves, your children,
And say, I have been dead a year or two;
How fondly am I living through their lives?
Go through them slowly, one by one by one.
Your friends recall you once or twice a year
To try the idiom of tenderness
Wherein you are no more than is a title
Set to a poem perfect in itself.
Your loves dared not to think of you a while,
And then they merely did not think of you,
And when at last in the gay resurrection
Nature reserves for those who have not died
They looked into new eyes and love bewildered

Their mortal boughs with burgeoning again,
How should they ponder over the dead leaves,
How should they turn away from the clear look
Of favor in the eyes of life, to brood
On dim reproaches in the eyes of death
Sunk in their skull beneath the drenching rain?
Your children have inherited your wealth,
The most persuasive comforter of woe,
Or else, perhaps, your poverty, and they
Speak never of you, lest too bitterly.
O sooner than the earth recalls its own,
Before the flesh unfastens from the bone,
The memory of you buried in the heart
Of one still living softly falls apart.
Your face upturned against the earth and rain
Outlasts the image of it in his brain;
Your phantom tread on stairways of his thought
Falters, recedes, grows fainter, and is gone.
Even your senseless immortality
Of grass rots in the rain.

                    But now you say
You hear your heart still ticking? You still live?
But listen closer, the beat fluctuates,
The arteries swell with uncertain pulse
And all within you, the corrupted highway
Of nerves and muscles, rutted and worn away
With traffic of your many joys and sorrows,
Glows lax in the foreboding of its end.

We come with leaden footsteps, we will wake
You under the midnight, we will wake you under
The midnight when the world has fallen away.
Life has receded from you like a tide,
Leaving the flats to view, where empty shells

Of dead experience echo the ebbing waves.
We will remember for you all your follies,
The bungled kiss, the passionate ineptness,
We will compute the garner of the years,
The eyes grown dim to color, ears to sound,
Nostrils to perfume, every nerve gone slack
To untune the instrument on which you played
Such gallant music for your little while.
We come with leaden tread, we come on leaden
Feet; you shall go with us, you shall go
With us down to the deeper caves of midnight,
While the unending rain falls on the earth,
Drumming on roofs, on pavements, on the graves
Of men who loved the warmth upon their hands,
And sweet sensations in a little room.
Listen! your heart is growing fainter, Listen!
It leaps once and . . . Listen! Only the rain
On midnight fields from which no harvest comes.

III. The Dream

WE ARE the dancers, we will dance
You over the mountain, we will dance you over
The mountain, we will dance you over the sea.
Our feet will flash before you among the crags
Or dart along the seaways. You will say,
The twinkle of sun is dazzling to my eyes.
—But listen! and you will hear the rainbow. Listen,
And you will hear us shout. Listen, and you,
Borne on that music, will slide sideways into
The air, your body itself will float in ether.
Perhaps you will say, I do not like this song;
It minds me of the swan who sings and dies,
Or of the swan who curses God and dies,

Or of the swan who sees Naples and dies,
Curses and sees, and dies. Or sings and dies.
—But lift out of the death. Lift with a song
Out of the death. Lift with the song of death!
Or perhaps you will say, be with me for this moment
Of ecstasy, and then begone, begone,
Lest I should see your face among the books
I read for my employment in the alley.
—Let us be tiger-hearted, let us be
Tiger-hearted, let us be suns of splendor,
Swift and sleek along the dewdrops of weeds
That scare the ploughman ploughing for lonely
       bread.
O coward, you have dreamed it! you have floated
Heavenward over the eyes of applauding friends.
Do you need a dream for flight? do you need a
       dream
To launch into the air aslant with yielding?
Do you need the plaudits of your friends to fly?
Take life then as a dream, take us for friends,
For we invisible are nimbler still
Than you, though you traverse the centuries
Full thirty cubits down Egyptian mould.
For we are wingless, being ourselves the wings.
We will applaud you, we will seize the crowns
Of Ætna and Vesuvius to fling
Across your orbit. We will make you proud
Knowing ourselves profundities of pride
And dream beyond your Romes and Arcadies.
Beneath our eyes the iron cities rust,
And kings show meanly in grey films of dust
On which the housemaid writes her name; we are
The light between the telescope and star,
Out-riding years of light. We fling ourselves
Into the void while constellations sing.

Snow falls on snow till worlds are buried in snow,
Flowers on flowers till deserts are paths of sand,
And oceans, pools in a garden too large for the
     heartbeat
Of any except two lovers when you are one,
Of any except two lovers when all are one.
Look not for our footsteps in summer unless you
     are clever
In charting the path of the wind on the leaves.
     Perhaps
In winter the swirl of our merriment brushing the
     snowdrifts
Will give you a pattern. Perhaps if you swim
     undersea
You will find, even fainter than tracks from the
     fin of a minnow,
The figures our swift minuet will inscribe on the
     sand.

We are the dancers. We dance glory
To you and to ourselves; our feet discharge
Long yellow flashes as of flint on steel
Between red Mars and white Aldebaran.
We are the glory, we are the dancers, you
Will dance with us, you will dance glory with us,
Over the mountain, over the ocean, over
The mountain, over the sea, beyond the mountain,
Beyond the mountain and the sea. Beyond.

iv. The Lovers

As IF with deep foreknowledge like the earth
Which murmurs spring before the spring is heard,
She slipped her hand in his and led him forth
Through secret ways that opened on a hill

Where the wind rippling up the grass sent waves
Of green to lose themselves against the sky,
And downward tumbled glittering waters, shouting
Of waterfalls and oceans yet to come.
The lovers wandered, neither daring now
One word of what their hearts were clamoring,
Until, his arm through hers, he turned her toward him
And face to face they trembled in the sunlight.

He whispered, "Are the eyes that dreamed so long
Of love afraid of love?" "They are not afraid,"
She answered, "they are dazzled with the sun."
"Let us throw off our dreams then; let us cast
Our fears away," he said, "as we threw off
Our garments; let us, naked of our past,
Climb up the flowery slope. Be now your heart
My heart, the quickening beat in both the song
Of lovers climbing hills in early morning.
Your breath that slumbered for the thousand years
And mine that battled with the wind are mingled
In the strong gasp of happiness prevailing
Yet for a swifter pulse and richer blood
To sweep through every vein; O may this hill
Not end, O may we never reach the crest
But like a bird that out of sight and hearing
Spirals upward in the ecstasy
Of death, mount to the sun. . . . O my Beloved,
Are you afraid?" "No, not afraid, not now.
Let us a while lie here in the long grass
And as our heartbeats slow to calmer pace
Still be their measure one. I fear only
That I should sleep and wake to find you gone,
Sleep for a thousand years, and find you gone.
Or else that death should come on one of us;
No, I am not afraid of love," she said.

He lifted up his hand and pointed far
Where range on range the blue hills fell away.
"Those lie before us, or before our children,
And we have passed beyond the fear of death
Who have passed beyond the fear of love. O never
Shall death come near us now. I can not tell you
Whether we still are on the whirling earth
Or far beyond it, unaware immortals;
I can not tell you whether we shall always,
You with your name and I with mine, go forth
To climb the hills before the dew has left them.
But if not we, our children; and if not
This love of ours, the same love born in them.
What more of everlastingness could gods
Ask than to behold their flesh renewed
In fairer bodies, and their old desires
Flowing from greener stems that are their own?
Happy were I to be as now forever,
But change is on the world and if we change
We shall but leave this to our fairer selves,—
The rest is but a love of little names."
But as he spoke she turned away from him
And gazed far down the slope whence they had come,
Back to the sleeping palace, and beyond it
The forest wrapped in fog, whence mournfully
Sounded the echoes of two bells. He smiled
Seeing she had not heard him, and was silent
Until a darker thought swam over him
Like clouds across the sunlight, and he shuddered.
"I seem to hear . . . was it two bells I heard?
Was it the slash of rain against the window
Before we died? Forgive me, I am strange
To credit happiness. I thought you dead
And would have gathered up the pitiful dust
That was your body, held it in my hand,

And breathing on it, blown my life away
For east or west to gather, autumn or spring.
I would have shed my years to stand beside you
Leafless, shed my hearing and my sight,
My thoughts, since you were no more to be heard
Or seen or thought of; yes, and before that
I can remember weariness of worship
In those few days of our companionship
When I consumed you utterly, and still
With the last atom of your excellence
Yearned for you more. I would have lost myself
Wholly in you, held nothing back, I would
Have been you only, though at last your dust
Was little on my palm." "Let death go by,"
She answered, "in the wind rustling the leaves,
Depart without departure, blow away
And still blow on, only its music lingering."
Then artfully and timidly, she asked him,
"During my thousand years of sleep where were you
Besides the broken dream I had of you?
I saw the sunlight chequered through the trellis
And would have asked that life go on for ever
With music and with toys and make-believe.
But suddenly I slept. Where were you then
Through all that pausing summer afternoon?
—Tell me, for I am jealous of the past."
"I too might well have slept. There is no story
Which is not you, Beloved. What befell me
Might befall any man. Perhaps I learned
More of deceit than most because I trusted
All men and women more than most. My friends
Betrayed me, women lied to me; and once
I swung my sword against reputed foes
Who when the fog of battle cleared away
Whispered with dying lips my brother's name."

"Peace, that is over. Tears for that dead sorrow
Would kill the living joy. Those countries now
Are less than dreams and the lost dreamers there
Have all forgotten you. Your friends remembered
Your name a while; your loves dared not remember,
But all are one now in forgetting you."
He laughed, "That was a dread I had at midnight,
Now it is like a cup of sunny wine
To lips that shuddered, thinking it of hemlock.
So long, so bitter, the weeping upon earth,
So short the hours under the drunken arbor
Where body and body search the plangent nerves
And find no answer to their loud demanding.
All have we done that mortal things can do,
We have been born, been loved, been slain and buried,
And still unsatisfied because our beauty
Is greater than we gave or could be taken,
We have done nothing, all has worked upon us,
Loved us too much and left us after love
In bondage of inaction. Not until
I put behind me the false loves which are
But vanity that feeds on adoration,
Not till I scattered them, their flatteries
Still mouthing on the air, and sought you out
Could I be sure that death and you were parted,
That dust was not a rival, that I could
Ride back and back through calendars of doubt
And find you in the end as in the beginning."

She said again, "These thousand years, where were you?
Tell me, for I am jealous of your past."
"Must I remember? there are planes of music
Which would bring back without an absent tinge
The little curtained room, the log fire burning,

And the old love, but all these moments knew
Themselves foredoomed, seeing within the crystal
Of their own ecstasy the grey forms gathering,
Cowled, with averted gaze, because their joy
Was but a song beleaguered by the silence.
There were no loves which were not you, Beloved.
Till now when I am healed, there was no time
I did not seek you to fulfill the dream
You had during your long sleep and forgot.
Before the world was; yes, before the thought
Of any world had sundered the great light
Into the rainbow, then we were together
And now we are together once again.
That is enough, O trust me! though you saw
Me prowling jungles of despair and lust
To mate with monstrous loves within my thought.
And I am here as one who finds redemption
Out of his earnings in another world."
"Shall I confess," she whispered, "that I dreamed
Without forgetfulness? But of that dream
I can not tell you all, nor any woman
Tell to any man. I saw you shaping
My image through so many others, saw them
The hateful and the beautiful, myself
In many forms adroit to do your pleasure
According to your will. For you I was
Savage and desperate under the wan moon,
I was the handmaid of your self-esteem
Or the deliverer from fear. I slept
Not peacefully who dreamed so many shames.
I could not waken to this happiness
Till you were weary of my counterfeits
And sought me out and bade me rise, myself,
None other, so made perfect in your love."

So faded the two lovers up the hillside,
And yet when they had seemed for ever vanished
They glimmered in the half-light as they passed
Over the fields between the scattered copses.
And when the veering wind blew straight across
From hill to hill, their voices floated back,
A murmured phrase, sometimes a gust of laughter.
And as the evening star rose clear before them
They reached the summit of the seventh hill,
Where lifted to a momentary glory
They stood against the sky, and so were gone.

LETTERS

A Letter to a Teacher of English *

Your learning, James, in classics and romance,
Sits lightlier than most men's ignorance.
It is yourself, an undivided part
Of you as man, not only mind but heart.
How often do I see in our profession
Learning a mere extraneous possession,
A self-sufficient mass of dates and sources
Roll'd round in academe's diurnal courses,
Where scholars prepare scholars, not for life
But gaudy footnotes and a threadbare wife,—
Keen eyes for errors in a worthless text,
But none at all for this world or the next.
I fall between two stools—I can't say Chairs—
A bard too learn'd, a scholar in arrears.
The critical reviewers, week by week,
Damn poets who command their own technique.
A careful rhyme, a spondee nobly planned
Is academic, and the work unmanned.
Would that these critics lived in houses fashioned
By carpenters congenially impassioned.
I'd love to see the rooftree fall on . . . no,
The name is legion; let us leave it so.
But as a teacher I have equal luck,—
In ponds a chicken and on shore a duck.
My wretched memory, for all my pains,
Drops tons for every ounce that it retains;
Far wiser now, I have less factual knowledge
At forty-one than when I was in college.

* Delivered as the Phi Beta Kappa poem at the Tercentenary of
Harvard College in 1936. The "teacher of English" is my friend,
Professor James Buell Munn, of Harvard. This is the second of
two Phi Beta Kappa poems delivered at Harvard. The other was
in 1928 and is not included.

With eyes astonished, I peruse the rant
My younger self delivered against Kant.
The *Critique of Pure Reason* was to me
Mere holiday from Greek philosophy.
The Greeks I can remember in due season,
But where now is the *Critique of Pure Reason?*
Alas, that educated men should find
Their memory not equal to their mind!
But since I have to choose, the lifeless fact
Must yield before the will to write and act.
Though I salute my past for what he knew
Let him return the bow for what I do;—
Thus to reverse, and much more truly say:
Si vieillesse savait, si jeunesse pouvait.

Yet there is recompense for knowing well
One language, if it be incomparable.
Disdainful, the Athenian would speak
No other language than his native Greek.
Now his provincial literature is prized
In every barbarous tongue that he despised.
The learned Roman, who knew Greek by heart,
Had twice the scholarship, and half the art.
The great Elizabethans' education
Thrived less on lore than on superb translation.
Our scholars, to whom every root is known,
Command all languages, except their own;
For confirmation, but consult the theses
That year by year bankrupt the college presses.

When poets go, grammarians arrive.
Is Virgil dead? Let commentators thrive.
The gift of tongues without the Holy Ghost
Is but a Babel, not a Pentecost.
Research in science may produce the answer

To love or wealth, to authorship or cancer;
Research in language? What is there to cure?
Some languages are dead and some endure,
Some fossil bones, some living literature.
Science in language is a game, designed
As rare Ben Jonson said, to break a mind;
One lives in words or knows them not at all
And weeps at the grammarian's funeral.
Romantic doctrine if you will, but who
Knowing his Gothic, knows his English too?
Mere English, mightiest tongue, whose cadences
Roar with the tides and murmur with the trees,
Since I hear living beauty, what care I
What tongues dared frame thy fearful symmetry?
I will not see thee petrified, my native
Language frozen to a fossil dative.
In short, dear James, by now you plainly see
I find no virtue in philology;
At best a sterile hobby, often worse,
The plumes, when language dies, upon its hearse.

Besides Illisus under the cool trees
Youth answered questions put by Socrates.
It does not matter what the questions were,
Suffice the youth and the philosopher.
Both, doubtless, would have thought it very odd
To trace the genitives in Hesiod;
Their works were intermingled with their days,
It was enough to know, not paraphrase.
Their voices reach me this calm afternoon
Through the bright air honeyed with ample June
More clearly than the meaningless confusion
That dominates the modern world's illusion.
Clearest of all, one question rouses me:
"Why have you lost the old simplicity

In life and learning, politics and art,
While wisdom, peace, and innocence depart?"

Though we who teach cry out against the mesh
Spread by the world, the Devil, and the flesh
To entrap the moneyed in material things
While we at lofty altitude spread wings,
Yet are we not materialists ourselves?
They build their mansions, we extend our shelves;
They flaunt possessions, we a weary text,
One-tenth original, nine-tenths indexed,
Both of us sharing in a common loss
Of life's essentials smothered by a gloss.

Now, James, I stop complaining, I will plan
An education to produce a man.
Make no mistake, I do not want this done,—
My limitations are the cornerstone.
Plato's *Republic* may have served some use
In manuscript, but not in Syracuse,
So let my dream Academy remain
A dream;—I'm sure I do not ask in vain.

First would I have my scholar learn the tongue
He never learned to speak when he was young;
Then would I have him read therein, but merely
In the great books, to understand them clearly.
At present, for no earthly good, we ask
A deadly and unnecessary task:
A knowledge of small names that time has taken
And put to bed—and whom we vainly waken.
O that our living literature could be
Our sustenance, not archaeology!
Time is the wisest judge, who folds away
The surplus of a too-abundant day.

My scholar shall be brilliantly forbidden
To dig old garbage from a kitchen midden;
Old it may be, and curious as old,
But I would have him dig for purest gold:
The text itself, no footnotes but his own,
And critics who let well enough alone.
Far better Alexandria in flames
Than buried beneath unimportant names;
And even Sappho, glory that was Greece's,
Lives best, I blasphemously think, in pieces.
Surely our sprite, who over Amherst hovered,
Would gain if no more poems were discovered.
That Chinese emperor who burned the books
Succumbed to madness shrewder than it looks;
The minor poets and the minor sages
Went up in smoke; the great shine down the ages.
The Harvard Library's ungainly porch
Has often made me hunger for a torch,
But this not more to simplify a lecture
Than to appease the Muse of architecture.

When music and sweet poetry agree,
Who would be thinking of a Ph. D.?
O who would ablauts bear, when Brahms's First
Is soon to be performed or but rehearsed?
My scholar must have music in his heart,
Bach and Beethoven, Schumann and Mozart,
Handel, Vivaldi, Purcell, Couperin,
Dowland, Corelli, Mendelssohn, Chopin.
Ah James, I missed my calling; I would turn
To that one art toward which the others yearn,—
But I observe my neighbor's cow, who leaves
Her fertile pasture for my barren sheaves.
The field next-door, the next-door art, will thus
Always attract the mildly covetous.

Yet some day I will play you the main theme
Of the immortal counterpoint I dream:
Clear melody in fugue and canon rises
On strings, with many structural surprises.
No letter, but a prelude, for your sake
I would compose beside this tranquil lake.
Its line should rise toward heaven until it broke
Half-way between the sky and the great oak;
Then waver, like a flock of homing birds,
In slow descending flights of minor thirds.
Music alone can set the spirit free
From the dark past and darker things to be.
I'd live for ever in an atmosphere
Of high harmonics where all tones are clear.
Could Man be judged by music, then the Lord
Would quench the angel of the flaming sword.
Alas, the final tones so soon disperse
Their echoes through the empty universe,
And hearers, weak from following Beethoven,
Relax with Gershwin, Herbert, and de Koven.

But to return to Polyhymnia,
And incidentally to my student. Ah,
Where is the creature? Nay, but is that he?
A saxophone is nuzzling on his knee!
His eyes pop out, his bellied cheeks expand,
His foot taps "Alexander's Ragtime Band."
Ungraceful and unpardonable wretch!
Was it for you my eager pen would sketch
A new, a sensible curriculum?
Burst with your panpipes! and we'll both be dumb.

I was about to urge philosophy,
Especially the Greek, I was to be
Your godfather in recommending Faith

To you, fit godson for a Sigmund Spaeth!
Of history and time I was to tell,
Things visible and things invisible,
But what to you are echoes from Nicaea,
Who never prayed nor cherished an idea?
And what have you to gain from education,
Blown bellows for unceasing syncopation?
Learning and life are too far wrenched apart,
I can not reconcile, for all my art,
Studies that go one way and life another,
Tastes that demoralize, and tests that smother.

James, what is this I find? an angry scowl
Sits on my brow like a Palladian owl!
Let me erase it, lest it should transform
The soft horizon with a thunder storm.
I would you were beside me now, to share
The sound of falling water, the sweet air.
Under the yew a vacant easy chair
Awaits your coming; and long-planted seeds
Begin to bloom amid the encircling weeds.
I bade my student an abrupt adieu
But find it harder to take leave of you.

May we not some day have a mild carouse
In Pontefract instead of Warren House?
The distance nothing,—in two hours' time
Another land where that word's but a rhyme.
Would I were Marvell, then you could not harden
Your heart against a visit to my garden.
I'd write those happy lines about the green
Annihilation, and you'd soon be seen
Hatless and coatless, bootless,—well, my soul!
He's in the lake with nothing on at all!
Farewell, and yours sincerely, and yours ever,

The time has come for the initial shiver.
When into lakes, as into life, we dive,
We're fortunate if we come up alive.

A Letter to Robert Frost *

OUR friendship, Robert, firm through twenty years,
Dares not commend these couplets to your ears:
How celebrate a thing so rich and strange—
Two poets whose affection does not change;
Immune to all the perils Nature sends,
World war and revolution and kind friends.
Something there is that doesn't love a wall;
Your apples and my pines knew none at all,
But grow together in that ghostly lot
Where your Vermont meets my Connecticut.
Ours is a startling friendship, because art,
Mother of quarrels who tears friends apart,
Has bound us ever closer, mind and heart.

Before the War, among those days that seem
Bathed in the slanting afterglow of dream,
Were happy autumn hours when you and I
Walked down that street still bright in memory.
I was a boy apprenticed to my rhymes,
Your fame already rose above our times,
Your shadow walking tall, my shorter gait,—
Both taller now, the difference as great.

Of wisdom I learned much, an artist's creed
Of work the flower, and worldly fame the weed;

* Delivered as the Phi Beta Kappa poem at Columbia University,
1936.

I have forgotten phrases; it remains
As part of me, it courses in my veins.
From many conversations I remember
One on a windy day in late November.
The sly recluse of Amherst in those times
Moved me, in spite of questionable rhymes.
We talked of women poets, nothing else,
From Sappho to our friend at Sevenels.
"Miss Dickinson is best!" You shook your head.
"Perhaps a genius, but mad," you said.
Alas for Emily, alas for me,
That now I go much further than agree:
Once irresistible, now sometimes coy,
Her whims, her verbal airs and graces cloy.
Taste changes. Candid Louis Untermeyer
Consigns his past editions to the fire;
His new anthology, refined and thrifty,
Builds up some poets and dismisses fifty.
And every poet spared, as is but human,
Remarks upon his critical acumen.

Ah, could we know what vogue will be tomorrow,
What plumes of Paradise our pens could borrow!
Or to the Communistic muse entrust
Our sparrow feathers ruffling in the dust.
You bid me name no names, so I shall heed
By using cypher he who runs may read.
In short, I note the vogue no longer smiles
On one un-Briton in the British Isles;
Nor heeds from Italy that "wandering voice"
Whose absence should make Idaho rejoice.
Ah, sir, commend me to your quiet wit
That smiles at fraud and so dismembers it.
These twenty years the precious frauds I've seen
Relieved themselves of gall—and me of spleen.

You with relentless patience watch them go,
My rage prolongs their stay a week or so.

Yet not alone among the modern names
Does Fashion choose; she rummages in Fame's.
One poet to be praised—and sometimes read—
She chooses, and the rest are safely dead.
One must be sacrificed if one is praised.
As Crashaw mounts, Shelley must be abased.
With what astonishment we witnessed Donne,
A poet we have always counted on,
Whisked from his niche among the second shelves
And placed with Chaucer, Shakespeare,—and our-
    selves!
While Blake departs, abandoned by the vogue,
To Beulah-land, where Reason is the rogue;
And Hopkins, Fashion's choice to follow Donne,
Rattling his rusty paeons, climbs the sun.
Blest be thy name, O Vogue, that canst embalm
A minor poet with a potted palm;
Make me immortal in thy exegesis,—
Or failing that, at least a Doctor's thesis.

Yet, Robert, through the charlatans who swarm
Like blowing gnats before the social storm,
The stout immortals stand in this our time,
With manners, morals, metres,—even rhyme.
Not every age can triumph over death
In the bright train of Queen Elizabeth,
And our ingenious and cynic age
Has not quite lost the better heritage.
Take Robert Bridges, laureate forever,
Calm as the sea and flowing as a river,
Who knew his source and end, but also knew
The homely country he meandered through;

Who, when we thought his broadening current spent,
Flung high that sun-capped wave, his Testament.
And Robinson, what other age but this
Has bred so classic an antithesis?
Mild in his manner, mocking in his eye,
Bold in appraisal, and in statement shy,
He knew all men,—the Man against the Sky.
And urbane Santayana, who alone
Among philosophers still seeks their Stone;
Whose irony, in golden prose alloyed
With doubt, yet yields not to the acid Freud;
Who after years of rightful fame defrauded,
Wrote one bad book at last,—and all applauded.

If gold get rusty, what shall iron do?
If poets, prophets, critics, are untrue,
Why blame the statesmen, who in turn reflect
On dusty mirrors the uncircumspect?
When poets laugh at metres, with applause,
Why punish citizens who laugh at laws?
All follies regimented are akin—
Free verse and Bolshevism and bad gin.
Surely a subtle spring, in flow or drought,
Waters one age or burns another out.
When worlds go mad, all things go mad together,
Nations, philosophers, the arts, the weather.
Beholding war, Nature, who brooks no rival
In blind destruction, threatens Man's survival.
While underground he plants his dynamite,
She answers with an earthquake overnight.
While from ingenious wings his bombs rain down,
She rips the clouds apart, and cities drown.
Machine guns clatter, but her ticking worm
Of death bombards his armies with a germ.
Nor can the propaganda of slow doubt

That one by one puts all Faith's candles out
Find Nature unprepared; her insect ranks
For Man's destructive unbelief give thanks.
The ant, the termite, and their brotherhood
Wait busily, as all good soviets should,
To crack his concrete and to gnaw his wood,
And, after war and storm have done their worst,
To view the last man, as they viewed the first.

From such dark thoughts only Dark Ages come;
I see not yet the end of Christendom;—
And if an end? In cloistered minds like yours
The classic wisdom of the past endures;
The ancient learning from the ancient guilt
Survives, and from slim chances worlds are built.
Black-armored barons, after Rome declined,
Warred on each other and on soul and mind;
Yet while they slept, cell after lonely cell,
Nearsighted eyes bent to the pliant quill.
The things that make outlive the things that mar,
Rome and Byzantium crashed,—but here we are.

Men are as cells within a mighty brain
Swept with one thought of happiness or pain;
Thus when the Thinker gazed beyond all time
Egypt and China blossomed at their prime,
Both worshipers of beauty and of peace.
That mood resolved. He meditated Greece,
Whose culture, wedded to the arts of war,
Brought beauty forth and slew the thing it bore.
Less fortunate we who brought forth the machine
And dare not slay it, lest the truth be seen
That we, now helplessly identified
With the machine, would perish if it died.
We watch each other, our fates intertwined:

It feeds us canned goods and we feed it mind;
It kills us and then calls us from the grave
With new machines, lest it should lack a slave.

In war, where no one wins but the machine,
I pondered as I brought the wounded in:
Of these three choices—death, deformity,
Or patched for war again, who would not die?
And now the final triumph: the star actor
In *Steel: a Tragedy*, makes God a tractor.
Yet let us still believe, in thinking deeper,
These are but twitchings of a troubled Sleeper
In whom the nightmare rages, and who can
To-morrow dream the incredible—a Man.

Why, Robert, look! it's after midnight. Always
At this hour I hear stirrings in the hallways.
You would not mind. If I recall aright
You and Miss Lowell would converse all night,
Seldom agreeing, always the best friends
That poetry can shape to different ends;
Myself, too sleepy then as now, would run
To catch the last car back at half-past one.
Heigh-ho, I've seen worse things than morbid youth
Inscribes in his dark diary. The truth
Remains that my few perfect moments seem
Eternal, and the bad ones but a dream.
Like Johnson's friend, I woo philosophy,
But cheerfulness creeps in in spite of me.
So does the spirit sift a life away
Into its best, preparing for the day
When, from its golden nucleus, shall rise
That happy part attuned to happier skies.

But happier skies? That phrase is fustian stuff,—
This green Connecticut is good enough;

My shining acres and the house I built,
All mine, all earned, all mortgaged to the hilt.
If I may make some changes here and there
When halos play on my unhallowed hair,
New England winters well might be curtailed—
In May it snowed, and in July it hailed.
And yet I shrink from this celestial boom,
Lest, with improvements, also I assume
Responsibility for things in bloom.
I might forget wax flowers of huckleberry,
I might leave out the fragrance of wild cherry;
In short, I hopefully resign to God
The natural world. O that our statesmen would!

And so good night with lullabye, my friend,
Republics fall and even letters end,
And Horace at one elbow sings of home
Far more eternal than the hills of Rome;—
And Gibbon, at my other elbow, gives
Wry testimony of what dies, what lives,—
A secret not to be imparted, but
Known to Vermont and to Connecticut:
New as to-morrow's dawn, old as the Nile,
In Nefertiti's tears and Shakespeare's smile,
And all so simple in an age of guile;
For Horace on his acres has no fears;
His empire grows through twenty hundred years.

Good night, I take unconscionable time
A-dying, but in rhymeless years a rhyme
Bids one converse beyond the crack of dawn,—
It now has cracked, and dew is on the lawn.
Since I write oftener than you, I vow
Another letter twenty years from now.

A Letter to My Son (1936)

BETWEEN us, Stanley, we must bridge a span
Perhaps the broadest in the life of Man.
McKinley and Victoria, familiar
As household gods when I was the young Hillyer,
To ashes and to legend have gone down,—
And Mickey Mouse has ousted Buster Brown,
In green suburban streets I played at ease,
Untroubled by the passing carriages,
Save when some dowager, averse to ball,
Scowled at us, brandishing her parasol,
Yet left (because of Grandmother) unspoken
Her thoughts of stolen grapes and windows broken.
Alas! though Mrs. Howe has been entombed
Some thirty years, my palate was foredoomed
Never again to taste such provender
As that forbidden fruit I stole from her.
I smell the arbors now, I see the lawn
Yellow with leaves like flakes of shattered dawn;
I smell the bonfire smoke, I smell the grapes;
But the October flavor still escapes.
I've planted twenty vineyards since that time
To catch the mixture of sweet juice and rime,
And not one grape, however cool and swollen,
Renews the ecstasy of those I've stolen.

It was a safe time, when all's said and done;
Backyards were big, streets open to the sun.
But sometimes, as if fashioned to disturb,
A horseless carriage pushed us to the curb;
Where teetering with fury, in full force
We shouted to the driver, "Get a horse!"
An incantation powerful enough
To stop the motor with expiring cough;

Whereat the driver, cursing as we jeered,
Beneath the underpinning disappeared.
O for the wisdom of those saucy boys
Who rightly guessed a danger in such toys,
Now toys no longer. With inverted roles,
Motors have made mere playthings of men's souls.
Not war, not plague, not any ill you mention
Has crushed mankind like this obscene invention;
All life resolves, in leisure or in toil,
To the production or misuse of oil.
Man's body flung full speed straight up the hill
Mounts with a nervous lift; his mind is nil.
Free in the air he skims, the while his spirit
Dives down to every ill that brutes inherit.
Let others praise inventiveness; I know
That where wings go there also bombs can go.
In short, dear son, my aging nervous centers
Quiver with indignation at inventors;
But you, no doubt, will find it commonplace
To speed through time and hurtle into space:
Two elements that bend to Berkeley's dream
By being something less than what they seem.
But though speedometers burn up with speed,
And clocks whirl madly at a moment's need,
Eternity awaits. That does not heed.

Yet I am not so much a misanthrope
As to conceive my past a future hope.
Things change, and that is well, and I am weary
Of the past gilded, and the future dreary.
Your childhood is just so much happier
As I am wiser than my parents were;—
Not to contemn them, but if sudden change
In common life swirls in so great a range,
Surely a loving and astute perspective

Ignores what once inspired a long invective.
And with it all, I would not seem to mock
My minute spent on the ancestral clock.
It was a nervous time, and I prefer
To split the seconds where they did not err.
Music I had and Christmas trees and books,
A sound physique and tolerable looks;
And something more, of undetermined cause,
That always irritates our best in-laws:
A calm, accumulated family feeling
That we survive though other clans go reeling,—
A sentiment that will annoy your wife,
But buttress you against the stress of life;
A doctrine not dependent on a name
Or the accoutrements of transient fame,
But adequacy quietly achieved,—
The right to live from those who rightly lived:
Farmers and judges, soldiers and professors,
Never the dispossessed or great possessors;
Avoiding, on the one hand, county farms,
And, on the other, bogus coats of arms.

How many honored names have played the fool
In social registers at boarding school,
Where youngsters form societies restricted
To lists of the elect and unelected;
A Calvinistic Judgment Day on earth,
Predestined by unworthy money's worth;
To sneer so natural, so unbent to laugh,
And calf love guided by the golden calf.
Soap-box or scented soap; the two extremes
Make nightmares of our democratic dreams.
That choice you must avoid; ay, there's the rub—
To join, but not exemplify, a club;
Or live on Grub Street and not be a grub.

I can not hope for you long years of peace;
Frail flies the halcyon from the shores of Greece.
Not long the tranquil sunlight, and not long
The sailors' cheerful chant, the pastoral song.
See, the waves turn to lead; the sun goes under
Thick looming cumuli alive with thunder.
For one false moment Nature holds its breath,
Then heights fall down, depths rise up from beneath.
In vain to furl the sail or guess the stars;
The storm that rends the hull snaps off the spars;
The rudder steers no course,—one aimless arc
And then the final dive into the dark.
Ships wood or steel, their captains fools or sages,
So they go, so men go, so go the ages.
And yet you still may read on empty graves
Where those should sleep who sleep beneath the waves:
"Sail thou! for even as we perished, we
Saw other ships sail on across the sea."
Let pale Lucretius from his sheltered coast
Rejoice in safety while the brave are lost.
Afraid of living as he feared the ocean,
He drank at last a love-inflaming potion
That killed Lucretius with his first emotion.

Dear son, if in this *pater filio*
I dare not gild the evils that I know,
Be not alarmed. Most generations think
Their world is trembling on the final brink.
My generation, nurtured on the pleasant
Illusion of a static world—that wasn't—
Woke with a start, both world and vision gone;
Yet better waking so, than dreaming on.
I'd gladly lap you in a Lydian theme,
But stronger music penetrates the dream,
The pulsing drum, the bugle, and the blast

That overthrows all ivory towers at last.
Go not to war except in your own heart,
To quell unreason and tear greed apart.
Take up your sword to guard that quiet gate
Against blind hatred in a world of hate.
Go not to war,—there's not a cause that gives
Life to the soldier who no longer lives.
No eloquence in how enduring stone
Makes unknown soldiers, to the future, known.
Go not to war! if Peace has lost her war
There is no other thing worth fighting for.
That dreamy Pharaoh who, beside the Nile,
Beheld the outstretched hands of morning smile;
When courier on courier cried for aid,
Let empires crumble, and was not afraid.
"Assyria mocks your honor. Babylon
Flames in revolt; your provinces are gone!
Send out your armies to maintain your pride."
The armies were not sent; the empire died.
Who cares to what dead sovereign it gives
Its dead allegiance? King Akhnaten lives!

Though life is perilous with war and wrack,
With fears that linger, loves that come not back;
Out of the fretted sea in after years
The slow-grown coral isle of joy appears.
I can not envy you your coming teens
That seize on life, not knowing what it means.
You in your first, I in my fifth, decade,
Perhaps are happiest when all is said.
But happiness so different, as to smother
Hopes of translating either to the other.
Yours is that rainbow web so finely spun
To catch the golden motes that dust the sun,
Floating along light air, a filmy skein

Torn by one gust or shattered by the rain.
But how shall I, to whom that joy is lost,
In memory's dull mirror find its ghost?
And how shall you, who know the shining thing,
Snare what is nothing if not on the wing?
Like gold, it goes as soon as you have felt it;
Time is the *aqua regia* to melt it,—
Time that brings love and debts and daily shaving;—
So spend the gold that vanishes with saving.

Now the November dusk is closing in,
The ink grows thick, the inspiration thin.
Time for your music lesson! Time for me
To fold the viewless wings of poesy.
Well-played, enrapt musician! I at nine
Had surely bungled that melodic line.
Play on, and happiness attend your song,
Sweet be its cadence, and its echoes, long.

A Letter to
Peyton Randolph Campbell
(Killed in Action, 1918)

You'll laugh, dear Randolph, to perceive that Satan
Has moved me to include the name of Peyton.
Well I remember the unreasoning shame
Your boyhood felt for that illustrious name.
I felt it for my middle name. We knew
How to annoy each other, as friends do.
"Peyton!" I'd shout, and "Silliman!" you'd cry,—
The fight was on, and fists began to fly.
I never walk down a suburban street
In autumn, when the blazing maples meet
Far overhead in tunneled radiance,
Without an unpremeditated glance
To find two little boys so hard at play
All life seems but an autumn holiday,
When the ripe grapes hang heavy from the vine
In shadowy arbors fragrant as old wine.

Life did not grant you much in days thereafter
But disappointments and the gift of laughter.
Some power must be, who accurately judges
To the last ounce how much the human drudges
Can carry, and then piles upon their backs,
Up to the breaking point, the futile packs.
You were a good man and you did good things;
And your reward? The shell, how shrill it sings!

A dubious reward, perhaps the best
For one who, finding evil, could not rest.
Evil enough there is, my lad, to keep
For ever aliens, your soul and sleep.

Perhaps more happy thus at twenty-four
To die, than struggle in this darker war,—
The spirit caught between the lines, the zero
Hour at dawn, where no dawn is, nor hero.

This drifting world needs men like you to man it;
I chide you for abandoning the planet.
Surely you might have dodged the shell, or better,
Persuaded with a diplomatic letter,
As others did, that you were valuable
Behind the lines, but not before a shell.
Alas, you yielded to your ruling vice,
A shameful lack of guile or cowardice.

You who were young, knew not when you were
     hurled
So suddenly, so brutally, from the world,
That you died vainly, and the truth you died for
Was but a sham that Englishmen had lied for.
You gave your life, as fine as it was short,
Not to your country, but the *Bryce Report,*
A document so void for sacrifice
It even, when the war was done, shocked Bryce,
Whose conscience bade him clear it off the slate,
A handsome disavowal—rather late.
But grown mature in spirit you may scan
Quite without bitterness that larger plan,
Where, nobly if mistakenly intended,
Your gift shall live when the last war has ended,—
A date that coincides, I greatly fear,
With Man's departure from this earthly sphere.

How shall we reach the dead? I can persuade
Your voice to echo back, or call your shade

Before me, as with wonted eagerness,
You bring me proof sheets from your printing press.
I can recall the little boy of four,
Or the young sergeant in the ancient war;
The adolescent scholar, the athlete,
His winged spirit swift in winged feet.
All those were you; now they are part of me.
My thoughts are not your immortality;
Thoughts never have been, they can never be.
Nor on this quiet morning do I look
For hints of you in wind or flower or brook.
Nature has business of her own—to live!
She has no immortality to give,
But feeds on life and death alike, nor cares
If it be Shakespeare or a flea she bears.

How shall we reach the dead? Shall it be thus:
A darkened room to awe the credulous,
A spiritistic circle, hand in hand,
A-sweat with visions of the Promised Land,
Whence, from the jasper walls and golden sheen
And gallant walks continually green,
Spirits return to thump a tambourine?
Our Lady sings *Magnificat* with tones
Surpassing sweet. These whistle "Casey Jones";
And, when consulted on immortal things
Divulge locations of lost wedding rings.
Far better the mute ashes of the Stoic
Then imbecilities so unheroic.
I can not hear the saints in sweet accord
Inscribing gibberish on a ouija board,
Nor flights of angels bearing to its rest
A table battered in a tipping test.
How shall we reach the dead? Are they reborn,

Bewildered mortals in a second morn?
Reincarnations whom the years discover
Unweaving and reweaving their lives over?
Disarmed of all experience, to make
The same small triumph and the same mistake,
Repeated through the ages, till they press
On to Nirvana, crowned with Nothingness?
Better a phantom universe than none,—
Anything, anything, but oblivion.
Reincarnation of the soul! of all
The theories, thou art the most logical,
A spiritual Darwinism, blest
By the huge shadow of Mount Everest.
From life to life ascending, spirits fashion
A gradual release from earthly passion.
Buddha, in whom all crude mutations cease,
Looms from the lotus, smilingly at peace;
The lotus flower at rest, the wheel of time
Stopped like a heartbeat from too high a climb.
Beneath that bending head, that dreamless face,
Time dies in an infinity of space.

Ah, vista of reincarnated lives,
Where no one less than king or queen survives,
How thou hast recompensed for lost romances
Old maids and wives in modest circumstances!
'Tis Cleopatra risen from the tomb
Who shines the pots and brandishes the broom.
I never yet have met the Christian slave,
But Queens of Babylon denude the grave.
Back from the past reenter, self-appointed,
More monarchs than the Lord could have anointed.

How shall we reach the dead?—Why should we
    reach them?
Just what have they to gain, or we to teach them?

Love is a bridge they may, perhaps, recross,—
Unwise, to drop in for an afterloss.
I can define the *here;* the *there* remains
A mystery unsolved, for all my pains.
The wise man, like Columbus, still prefers
His course unblurred by bad cartographers.
Sail West. Though India was your intent,
Accept, O valiant, a new continent,
Uncharted in the logic of the mind,
A faith not to be named, much less defined.
Prove it? Subjected to the earthly laws
Of reason and equation, faith withdraws.
Transcendent, it is an experience
Beyond the net of thought, the thrill of sense.
At intervals unheralded, it flows
Through all the being, and that moment knows
Eternity; its altitude goes out
Beyond all ages in an age of doubt.
Nor can belief by unbelief be bribed
To prove what can not even be described.
Far better so; we can not pass our days
Beneath the sun, blind from the fiercer blaze.
I have no patience with the so-called mystic
Who lives on crusts and symbols kabbalistic.
Yeats and his comrades in the Celtic dusk
Throw out the kernel and enjoy the husk.
The real conviction is austere and sharp;
A clear, high tone,—not an Aeolian harp.
It dies, but let us not in depths of night
Ever deny that we have seen the light.

And I will not permit one world to smother
My absolute conviction of another.
Perhaps the Universe, like Nature, seeds
Its garden many times beyond its needs.

It may be, as the wise Egyptians taught,
Some are immortal seed, and some are not.
Spirits have privilege of suicide;
I've seen them die before the body died,
The soul cut off from the immortal air
By lust or greed or cynical despair.

But in your heart, no evil thing could enter.
Your being, Randolph, from its radiant center,
Glowed through misfortunes beyond your control
That would have darkened a less manly soul.
I hesitate. In all our mortal days
We never once exchanged a word of praise!
How shy is youth, how strangely reticent,
So long withholding words we always meant!
But take them now, old friend; translate them better
Than earthly phrase affords this random letter.
Now through the mist, the Sunday morning bell
Rings murmurously over Woodstock hill.
Sanctus! the bell intones, and *Sanctus!* I
Deep in my wayward spirit make reply.
Therefore with angels and archangels, all
The company of Heaven lift the pall
From the dead past, and like a sudden shout
Across deep valleys, the bright sun comes out.

Peyton! farewell from Silliman! God knows,
I'd love to see you though we came to blows.

Excerpt from A Letter to Charles Townsend Copeland: Le Baron Russell Briggs

As DUSK comes on, I almost hope to meet
Dean Briggs once more in the familiar street,
His head thrown back, his amiable walk
Timed equally to progress or to talk.
I, whom life changes with its every whim
Remember now his steadfastness. In him
Was a perfection, an unworldly grace,
Life could not mar and death can not efface.
I know the wrinkled smile, the kindly eyes,
Keen with a wit both humorous and wise,—
These I remember, and remembering, see
The Dean walk home toward Immortality.
The Dean walks home, his cheerful task complete;
He walks at dusk down the familiar street,
Stopping to share some story with a friend,
Or murmur words of counsel. At the end
He pauses for a moment, and with shy
Farewell looks back, looks back and says Goodbye;
Then rounds the corner of his shining days,
His smile at parting bright through April haze.

LYRICS AND
SHORTER POEMS · III ·

The Relic

A MURMURING in empty shells
Recalls the ocean's undertone,
But not a wisp of music dwells
In this small skull of dulcet bone—
A thrush's skull, miraculous
Among dead leaves and threads of ice,
This delicate contrivance was
The sounding board of Paradise.

Beneath the tree lies music's skull,
The tree a skeleton of spring,
And both, perhaps, are beautiful
Though leaves and thrush no longer sing;
But, growing old, I have a reason
For wishing some divine delay
Could hold a song beyond its season
And hide the thrush's skull away.

Intermezzo

BY THE lake the orchards lie
Half in shadow, half in sun.
We were mortal, you and I;
We were parted. Now, as one,
We leave the shadow for the sun.

When I died I walked away
Down a long suburban street
Where the feathery elms of May
Arched as in a forest aisle.

There I walked as evening fell
Knowing that we two would meet
When the sickle moon was curled
Round the windmill by the well.

And you whispered with a smile,
"If you waken, you will weep;
That was in another world;
Now lie down, lie down and sleep."

Princess, if the lakes were dry,
And the orchard paths were frozen,
Would you still, unchanged as I,
Choose the lover you have chosen?

Scherzo

THE flower-girl, singing, comes up from the river,
Up through the field to the street of the village,
Bringing her basket heaped high with the pillage
Of riverside violet, lily, and rush.
The rays of the morning flicker and quiver
Warm on her arms and her glistening face,
And twinkle on anklets that jangle together
With tinkle of bells and melodious jingle
As gay as a robin and clear as a thrush.

The wind is awake with her, fingering ribbons and lace
That flutter in tatters, bright like a paradise feather;
The wind is awake with her up from the river so early
With songs that are part of the sunrise and mingle
With the singing of birds in the willow.

The herdboy has lifted his curly head from the pillow
Of grass at her singing;

And bows to her mockingly, makes a grimace,
And laughs to the laughter that ripples her face
Till the hillside is ringing.

Wind, wind, all night through the Emperor's gardens
You gathered the weary delight of the wise and the
   witty
And perfume that curled out of urns of gold.
Wind, all night through the city
You gathered the word that murders, the whisper that
   hardens
The minds of men in a horrible mould.

Scatter the cargo you gathered, and blow through the
   hair
Of the flower-girl singing at dawn through the street;
Scatter the cargo you gathered, and bear
The silvery laughter that rings from the hill.

I have opened my window. Pour over me; spill
All the spring at my feet!

Time

SUDDENLY it is upon you. Your tall sloop
Takes care of you as you took care of her,
And conscience says, "Whatever have I done?"

This is no time to let self-pity stir;
Your glands mean nothing to Aldebaran,
Nor can old dogs set sail for Guadeloupe.

Time passes. Time is past. And yet to sit
With sick eyes gazing at the unanswering world
Would be to invoke all that you have abhorred.

Leave something to fair Nature, amply stored
With morning glories' heavenly blue unfurled—

Leave something to good luck and to the Lord,
Knowing that, after all, they have the wit.

Dance

IF EVERYTHING were plentiful—as I would have it be—
You wouldn't have a thing to do but dance around the tree.
You think that you'd get tired of dancing in a round,
But that's because you don't know the kind of tree I've
     found,
The kind of tree that changes shape and season all the time,
A maple tree, a white oak, a rowan tree, a lime,
An acacia, an apple tree, a peach tree, a cherry,
In blossom, in leaf, or bare as February.
An ash tree, an elm tree, a sycamore, a birch,
Smaller than a sapling or taller than a church.
A walnut, a hickory, a mulberry, a quince,
A rose tree for the Princess, a cedar for the Prince.
And when your day was ended and the fiddlers all had
     stopped,
You'd want to go on dancing round the tree until you
     dropped.
"It only seems a moment now it's over—please go on!"
Save something for another day, dear child. The dance is
     done.

The Horsetail

THE spindly weed named horsetail (I can see
Small reason for the name) was once a tree

Aeons ago, so huge its upper boughs
Were lost in vapors from the reeking sloughs.
The pterodactyl, with a raucous scream,
Flapped to its jointed branches through the steam,
Witless of Nature's simple and succinct
"Reduce your stature or become extinct."
Alone amid that monstrous arboretum,
The philosophic horsetail (*Equisetum*)
Shrank through millenniums, until it stood
Twelve inches high amid another wood.

Surviving modestly, today it sees
The final humbling of ancestral trees,
Whose affluent decay from ancient soil
Is pumped by derricks ravenous for oil—
A million years of verdancy refined
To verdant millions of another kind.
The thin, ascetic plant, still running rife,
Deathless through trimming its demands on life,
Achieves its green, perennial intent;
While on vain errands or destruction bent,
My own coevals through the reeking sky
Like witless pterodactyls clatter by.

Lunar Moth

FROM the forest of night
Cometh the light
Green-wingëd flight—
Titania come
To a mortal's home
From the low-moon land
With her wings and her wand
And her bright black eyes

And her tiny feet
And her wings pale green
Like wind through wheat.
Now I am wise,
For now I have seen
Men told no lies
Of a fairy queen.
She was here on the wall,
And now she has gone,
Quiet, small,
To the night, alone.
With a wave of her wand
She vanished, beyond
The sky to the cool
Moon of July.

For Maister Geoffrey Chaucer

A BARD there was, and that a worthy wight,
Who, from the time that he began to write,
Served God and beauty with an humble mind,
And most of all he knew and loved mankind.
Laughing he was, and quick at many a jest,
The Lord loves mirth,—the devil take the rest!
A simple grace ere wine be poured at dinner,
A ready hand outstretched to saint and sinner,
A prayer at times, not lengthy but devout,
This was out poet's faith without a doubt.
Travel he loved, and wonders had to tell
Of royal France and Italy as well,
And everywhere he went, his furtive pen
Took down the secrets of his fellow men,
Their faces and their stories, high and low,
From lordly Petrarch and Boccaccio

Unto the meanest villein who could hold
A tavern audience with the tales he told.
But with his scrivening, he never swerved
From duty to the three kings whom he served,
And though he roamed both France and Italy,
England was where he always longed to be,
And thither he returned with magic spoils
That England might have pleasure of his toils,
And hear his brave, chivalric stories sung
By English pilgrims in the English tongue.
Noble his spirit was, and gay his heart.
A judge of wine, a master of his art,
He loved all men, nor was ashamed to show it;
He was a very parfit gentil poet,
Gentil in life and parfit in his rhyme,—
God send us such another in our time!

Eppur Si Muove?

ALTHOUGH it may appear archaic,
My cosmic system's Ptolemaic,
The earth for center, round which run
The circumnavigating sun,
The stars, the galaxy, the moon,
The planets, in concentric tune
To music of the spheres, that plucks
Notes in the theme of *Fiat Lux*
From every heavenly body bound
In counterpoint of radiant sound,
To merge in silence at the end,
Just as in white all colors blend.
And since I know I see but darkly,
I quite agree with Bishop Berkeley—
All is illusion—and I'd therefore

Choose the illusion I most care for.
   Nowise, so it seems to me,
Is happiness or dignity
Advanced by thinking earth is spun,
A mote of dust, around the sun
As sly Copernicans attest
From facts illusory as the rest
And in observed results more dreary
Than any other cosmic theory.
   Ah no, we sit, the earth and I,
While day and night go wheeling by,
The focus of attendant spheres
And keystone of the arching years.

Clear Melody

TREES in this November night
Are leafed with light
From street lamps, or the moon.
And you shall soon
Walk from the city to the wood
Where stood your birthplace, centuries
And centuries ago.

All moonlight, now; no snow, no nerves;
No avenues, one path that curves.

How can November thus
Be summer? fact be fabulous?
Bare boughs in leaf, dead grass in bloom?
You read the words on your own tomb,
By moonlight read the words and laugh
To read your epitaph.

While soft as a feather, soft as snow,
Or snowy moonlight on moonlit eaves,
One cricket weaves the winds together.

Sleep, you are there,
Sleep, you are home.
The moonlight comb
Combs your hair.
And now you are home.
After centuries, now.
After centuries, home.

Moo!

SUMMER is over, the old cow said,
And they'll shut me up in a draughty shed
To milk me by lamplight in the cold,
But I won't give much for I am old.
It's long ago that I came here
Gay and slim as a woodland deer;
It's long ago that I heard the roar
Of Smith's white bull by the sycamore.
And now there are bones where my flesh should be;
My backbone sags like an old roof tree,
And an apple snatched in a moment's frolic
Is just so many days of colic.
I'm neither a Jersey nor Holstein now
But only a faded sort of cow.
My calves are veal and I had as lief
That I could lay me down as beef;
Somehow, they always kill by halves,—
Why not take me when they take my calves?
Birch turns yellow and sumac red,
I've seen this all before, she said,

I'm tired of the field and tired of the shed.
There's no more grass, there's no more clover;
Summer is over, summer is over.

Dead Man's Corner, Verdun

HERE is the crossroads where the slain
Were piled so deep we could not pass.
Now dreams alone renew the stain
Of blood long soaked into the grass.

"Doucement; doucement!" I hear
The wounded gasping through their blood;
The ambulance with grinding gear
Lurches in shell-holes, sinks in mud.

If ambulance to save the maimed
Or gunwagon to maim the sound,
Both must proceed, while rightly named
The Mort Homme darkens all the ground.

As long ago wheels took the groove
In necessary roads again,
Crunching the bones that could not move
To move the limbs of wounded men;

With cracked and beaten lips that taste
Commands like acid but obeyed,
We still with leaden nightmare haste
Convey our shadows through the shade.

The Suspended Moment

WHAT do those stolid trees whose umber shoulders
Rise beyond corn shocks listen for, as though
They would step forward from among the boulders
Their roots have split, and move without a sound
At some expected signal from the sky?
The sun has set, and all behind them lie
The piled-up embers of the afterglow,
And sudden chill arises from the ground.

Who is that standing shadowed by the trees,
Almost invisible where field meets glade?
This evening trembles with expectancies;
Amid lifelong, unreasonable contrition
I am afraid of time and of time's ending,
As though the luminous evening now descending
Were the world's last. I am afraid, afraid
Of the dark plunge to endless repetition.

That was the child's dream, the black, cliff-like mirrors
Repeating and repeating death and birth
Till, paralyzed with individual terrors,
He cried out for forgetfulness once more
And woke in the assuaging arms of night
As I do now; all outlines put to flight,
Except my hands, dim moths of air and earth,
Praying the prayer I dared not pray before.

Barcarolle

THE long stems of the water lilies
tangle the paddle; the canoe
held among lotus and amaryllis
halts in the water garden. Few

are the birds in the trees that ring the pool;
only the hermit thrush still sings
in the unfathomed depth of cool
greenery fresh from hidden springs.
Few are the birds, and quite alone
is the man amid the summer maze,
adrift on this remote lagoon
as though eternity were his.
Perhaps it is; he may have passed
beyond the flickering of days.
Into a peace profound as this
the pebble of his heart was cast.

The Uprooted

WHEREVER wealth takes up its brief abode
Antiques come rolling down the open road;
Truckloads of furniture in endless lines
Follow the signposts toward the dollar signs,
The handicrafts that fashioned them forgotten,
The roofs that sheltered them caved in and rotten.
These humble chattels of our forebears stood
In Newport once, and then in Hollywood,
And now, where tax-free oil provides a palace,
They make their weary pilgrimage to Dallas.

Spindle and spokes at rest, the spinning wheel
Stands idle next to its companion reel,
Still able to prepare the homespun wool
But fated to be quaint and beautiful.
The prices paid for lustre would have bought
The whole establishment where it was wrought.
A cradle rocks the kindling wood to sleep,
The banjo clock has no more time to keep,

And unancestral portraits look askance
On those who bought, yet claim, inheritance.

Soon will the wealth move on, we know not where,
But this we know—the antiques will be there,
Proving that those who chase the future cast
Acquisitive back glances toward the past,
Where, in the objects of a simpler age,
Fancy, at least, can find a heritage.
So dowagers evoke the sixteen-eighties
With someone else's *lares et penates,*
Which, now grown skeptical of hearth and home,
Whisper all night of travels yet to come.

Night Piece

THERE is always the sound of falling water here;
By day, blended with birdsong and windy leaves,
By night, the only sound, steady and clear
Through the darkness, and half-heard through
　　　sleepers' dreams.
Here in the mottled shadow of glades, the deer
Unstartled, waits until the walker is near,
Then with a silent bound, without effort is gone,
While the sound of falling water goes on and on.

Those are not stars reflected in the lake,
They are shadows of stars that were there aeons ago;
When you walk by these waters at night, you must
　　　forsake
All you have known of time; you are timeless, alone,
The mystery almost revealed, like the breath you take
In summer dawn before the world is awake,
Or the last breath, when the spirit beyond recalling
Goes forth to the sound of water for ever falling.

Swift as deer, half-thoughts in the summer mind
Flash with their hints of happiness and are gone;
In the dark waters of our selves we find
No stars but shadows of stars which memory lost.
Dark are the waters under the bridge we crossed,
And the sound of their falling knows neither end
          nor start.
Frail are your stars, deep are your waters, mind;
And the sound of falling water troubles my heart.

Under Yonder Beech Tree

THE weeping beech tree forms a leafy cave
Cool as the hollow in a breaking wave;
There in a hammock made of woven mesh,
Mrs. Moran lays down her weary flesh.
The summer murmur, resonant and deep,
Vies with the shadows in persuading sleep.
Her pretty hands, her face as delicate
As shell, her feet too dainty for her weight,
All, frail as Dresden, seem not quite designed
With Mrs. M's anatomy in mind.
While appetite quells vanity, she dreams
Not of a lover but of chocolate creams.

One word might yet arouse her sense of duty
To trim the expanding pedestal of beauty,
But let it go unsaid. On sun-drenched days
The ghost of Gauguin or Gaston Lachaise
Might find in such heaped indolence of mood
A masterpiece of tropic amplitude.
Beauty is in the eye of the beholder:
Though she accumulates below the shoulder,
Mrs. Moran, asway in massive calm,

Suggests Tahiti and the coco-palm—
Full summer ease in one exotic touch
Amid a world that diets overmuch.

Fields in November

THE moon on these withered fields,
The pale, transforming light,
Gives them a glimmer of green,
The ghost of a summer night.
Long, long ago, it seems now,
When men were young in this land
Where nobody ever dreams now,
Except for the moon, there was magic
Over the world, and the path
Was open to south and north,
Till the wrinkled angel of wrath
Forbade that a man go forth
To the sun or the moon as he chose,
To the garden where he arose,
Or the mountain of silent snows.
I, like the rest, have lost much
Of my sight, hearing, and touch;
And I look on the breathing fields
In the glow of the moon and wonder
Where it has gone, that magic
Which led to the path beyond,
Where a man could be merry in spring
Forever, or sleep like a king
On the mountain of frozen thunder.

Scenic Railway

STRAPPED in our seats on time's great roller-coaster,
We are pulled slowly up through autumn haze,
Through winter chill, until late February,
When, with a brightening view of warmer days
We pause an instant on the breathless summit,
Then downward in accelerating glide
Through spring and the green-tunnelled summer plummet,
The sea on one side, flowers the other side—
Crocus to morning glory to the amber
Chrysanthemum frost-silvered in November.
Then under darkening skies we start the climb
All over, dreading the foreshortened hours
Of sunlight shrinking to pinpoints of time
And the frost silvering us like autumn flowers.
So have I ridden sixty turns and more—
My ancestors apparently lived well
To leave so many tickets at the door.
How many still are left? I will not dwell
On that or on the exit into dark
When, all my rides being over, I confront
The man who runs the whole amusement park,
And hear the inevitable "Do you want
Another batch of tickets, Mister?" What
Shall I reply to that? Do I—or not?

Bobwhite

THROUGH hottest days the bobwhite sings;
His two-toned, reedy whistle rings
Windblown, familiar on this lawn,
Or to remoter green withdrawn,
At one with evening as with dawn.

His other name, the quail, suggests
Gunshot and slaughter-emptied nests;
The squinting eye, the flabby grin,
As the curst hunter closes in.

Bobwhite—I call him what he calls
Himself, though often he'll repeat
The first of his cool syllables
As though to quench the summer heat—
Small sun-defier, to whose golden
Note my summer is beholden.

Incantation

CREATURES in the modern novel
Slink from cabin into hovel,
Dragging with their weary selves
Druggëd girls and draggled elves.
Give me pick and give me shovel,
Let oblivion's lower shelves
Deep in shale where no one delves
Bury them; below the levels
Known to mice or men or devils
Where the vampire weakly wails
When his heart is plugged with nails,
In unconsecrated gravel
Where no critics praise or cavil,
Where no royalty avails
From publicity or sales,
Take the psychopathic drivel,
Dying whine, infected snivel—
Though it won a brief approval
It is time for its removal.

Give me pick and give me shovel
To enter the modern novel.
Thanks . . .
                    What's that? Do you insist?
Good! Throw in the novelist.

The Survivors

BLEST be the bric-a-brac that still survives
Demolished houses and forgotten lives,
And, with a Dresden glimmer from the shelves,
Calls back the children who were once ourselves.
The French clock swings the mercury of time
Captive in glass and regular as rhyme.
The candelabra in their crystal lustres
Splinter a beam of light in rainbow clusters.
Swans die in their own music, roses in
Their own perfume, but roses from Pekin
And swans from Sèvres, having no scent or song,
Stay, while a hundred summers glide along.

Lovers from Meissen, clowns from Copenhagen,
Amorous cupids, innocently pagan,
Berribboned shepherds with their shepherdesses
Poised in forever-unachieved caresses:
These beings, like ourselves, were shaped from clay,
But in such heat as burned their lusts away.
Frozen in flame, they glazed to chilly fire,
Immune from death and death's pale twin, desire,
Unless, on some dyspeptic morning, Sadie's
Wild duster tangles in the porcelain ladies,
Or Mrs. Fulsome, clumsy connoisseur,
As usual breaks what most appeals to her.

Tiffany glass, they tell me with a smile—
In fact, all *art nouveau*—is back in style.
The eighteen-forties, too, come in for praise,
Late Empire, and my opalescent vase,
Which makes me wonder where such things would be
If Style had swept the previous century.
The architect, to serve the vogue, uptilts
Greenhouses thirty stories high on stilts,
Supplanti   stone with sheets of glass.
Like "Ge   hansard these will pass,
While,   anging, will remain
The on   —of porcelain.

‎e Guesses

B   n trees three little girls
S   ing, far away and hazy.
"   h, shaking out her curls;
        et said. "You are both crazy,"
        Druids all died long ago,
        tream. Those men are tramps, too lazy
        et too nervous to stay still."

        n parted halfway up the hill,
        ght out a grove, remote and dim,
        is Druid knife cut mistletoe.
One reached a river where he fished till dark.
The third one, setting all the dogs to bark,
Tramped on until the starlight cradled him.

Edith lay long awake that night and pondered.
Violet dreamed of rivers far away.
Jane, weaving endless computations, wondered
How much she could save up by New Year's Day.

The Suburb by the Sea

HERE, in the suburb by the sea, the surf
Foams on the rocks that guard the private turf,
And in flood tides of autumn does not halt
But pours across and sows the lawns with salt,
To break against the walls of terraces
Where Roman gardens and Shakespearean trees
Embower the mansion and the formal hedge
From all directions but the water's edge.
How beneficial are the rich, whose pride
Pays for this ornamental countryside,
A park that otherwise had vanished hence
Or been maintained at government expense.

The pocket harbor floats the local tanker
And is so flecked with gleaming yachts at anchor
That, from afar, observers might suppose a
Tree had shed white leaves on Vallombrosa,
Until the yachts, to change the simile,
Spreads wings like waterfowl and fly to sea.
Like birds, they migrate when the cold winds blow
And early winter dusts the air with snow.
The ice puts out, beneath the frosted moon,
A tentative webbed foot on the lagoon,
And mothers, to place debutantes on view,
Sublease a duplex on Park Avenue.

The suburb, ringed by housing projects, levelled
By taxes, and by satirists bedevilled,
Defaced by trade's encroaching sabotage,
Will shortly seem a lingering mirage.
With eyes that cherish what must soon expire,
I see it drift toward Nineveh and Tyre,
Its "Private Property—No Thoroughfare"

Shaken by city traffic roaring near.
No funds will serve, no sentiment avail,
To curb the influx from beyond the pale.
But after us the deluge! I shall be,
By then, in suburbs by a darker sea.

Nocturne

IF THE deep wood is haunted, it is I
Who am the the ghost; not the tall trees
Nor the white moonlight slanting down like rain,
Filling the hollows with bright pools of silver.

A long train whistle serpentines around the hill
Now shrill, now far away.
Tell me, from what dark smoky terminal
What train sets out for yesterday?

Or, since our spirits take off and resume
Their flesh as travellers their cloaks, O tell me where,
In what age and what country you will come,
That I may meet you there.

Never Fear

NEVER fear the phantom bird
Meditating in the Fens;
Night will come and quench your eyes,
Blind at last like other men's;
Never fear the tales you heard
In the rhetoric of lies.

Nothing here will challenge you,
Not the heron, tall and white,

Countersign upon the edge
Of the waterfall of night.
This is Avilon's canoe,
Eden murmurs in the sedge.

Here! my hand in pledge of rest.
Drift at random, all is well.
Twilight is a slow lagoon,
Dark will be a citadel.
Travellers who know the west
But report the waning moon.

In the citadel of peace
Hang the trophies of the world,
Yet no barons don their mail,
And no pennant is unfurled.
Daily robe, the Golden Fleece,
Daily cup, the Holy Grail.

Nightfall Bay

THE wind went with the sun. Two yellow stars
Like daffodils hang from the sickle moon.
Now evening's salty fingers probe the scars
Of memory, but sleep will heal them soon.
The hill-ringed bay, remote, unvisited
But by this glimmering, white sloop, is balm
To him who found no peace until he fled
From human turmoil to primeval calm,
And now stands, leaning slack against the mast,
Watching his cigarette smoke drifting gray,
While phantoms from his overcrowded past
Come back from years ago and miles away.
How still it is! The echo of a sigh
Makes the trees tremble on reflected sky.

In the Baroque Room

Poor Mr. Brummell, now grown middle-aged,
Is seldom pointed out and never paged.
Indignantly unrecognized he sits,
And blames the disappearance of the Ritz.
He broods on High Society brought low,
The smart Four Hundred scattered long ago,
Cotillions under crystal chandeliers
Before his time but not beyond his tears,
And days when Mrs. Astor's golden name
Touched Ward McAllister's to gilded fame.
Last night's gardenia in his neat lapel
Grows yellow with a faint, funereal smell.

When he was young, he was considered pensive,
Somewhat poetical but not offensive,
Until he chose a course that, as a rule,
Is left to women and to ridicule:
Social ambition, to whose shaky rung
Quite high, but not quite high enough, he clung.
Now silhouetted in the sunset casement,
He will not make his bow of self-effacement
Until he's summoned to that last cotillion
For the Four Hundred—and four hundred million,
Where Mrs. Astor's marble name confers
No light at all on Ward McAllister's.

Folk Song

The stars came, but her Love came never,
And standing there on the bank of the river,
"Come back!" she said to the waves of the river,
But they hurried away and they came back never.

"You come not back to the land of my lover,"
She said to the hurrying waves of the river,
"Then will I go with you, waves of the river,
To oceans far from the land of my lover."
Under the starlight the girl and the river
Hurry away and they come back never.

An Acquisition

In Muse's Bookshop, at the very back,
I purchased for ten cents a book of verse
To save the poet and that "Cousin Jack"
Whom he regarded warmly in a terse
Inscription on the flyleaf, from disdain;
Only to find that Cousin Jack had shed
Three other volumes by the family bard,
Each in its paper cover still unread,
And each presented with "my warm regard,"
Presented, dated, signed—all quite in vain.

I put down three more dimes and bought the lot:
This poet, long ago, had been my friend
As far as he was able, which was not
Much farther than the gaining of an end—
But memory has no need to judge the dead.
Going back ten years, I can see him sicken;
Going back twenty, proud and climbing high;
Going back thirty, pitifully stricken
With first experience of love's perfidy.
And, for my part, there's no more to be said.

And Cousin Jack? He must have been a savage
To sell these to a second-hand bookstore,
Where vulgar and philistine eyes could ravage

The metaphysics and the metaphor
That clutched at fame but chased the vogue too hard.
Yet maybe Cousin Jack is dead himself,
And all his books are in the bargain basement.
Well, there's an end. I'll put these on the shelf
Where, if I clip the ivy from the casement,
The sun will penetrate with warm regard.

Autumn Mooring

IN THE autumn a man needs a home;
    He may sail the summer away,
But when leaves fall and cold winds come
    And the steel-white day
When the northeast wind is at large in
    The ruined sky, when the shock
Of the sea shakes the foaming margin
    Of murderous rock;
Then he turns his back to the storm
    And crosses the lawn to his door
And steps inside, and is warm
    To the very core.

Lullaby

THE long canoe
Toward the shadowy shore,
One . . . two . . .
Three . . . four . . .
The paddle dips,
Turns in the wake,
Pauses, then
Forward again.

Water drips
From the blade to the lake.
Nothing but that,
No sound of wings;
The owl and bat
Are velvet things.
No wind awakes,
No fishes leap;
No rabbits creep
Among the brakes.
The long canoe
At the shadowy shore,
One . . . two . . .
Three . . . four . . .
A murmur now
Under the prow
Where rushes bow
To let us through.
One . . . two . . .
Upon the shore,
Three . . . four . . .
Upon the lake,
No one's awake,
No one's awake,
One . . . two . . .
No one, not even you.

xxth Century

THERE is no time,
No time,
There is no time,
Not even for a kiss,
Not even for this,
Not even for this rhyme.

It is May
And blossoms sway
In sifted snow
Under the moon.
I only know
That I can not stay,
For today is May
And tomorrow June.

An arrow shot
From an idiot's bow,
That is my lot
And I must go.

There is no time,
No time,
There is no time,
Not even for a kiss,
Not even for this,
Not even for this rhyme,—
        No . . . !

Resurgent

BETWEEN two worlds, caught!
The world that can be bought,
And the one too long unsought.

Like winter shoveling out
From under drifts, I, stout
With dayspring, shake off doubt.

What is it I have found?
Roots rich in the warm ground?
Breath free? Free wings unbound?

God whom the child knows? Soul
Recaptured? Heart made whole?
Gate open without toll?

There is a key that's worth
Just what you learn of Earth
From the moment of rebirth.

I am too tremulous now
To tell you where or how,
But the frown is off my brow,

The greed is off my hands;
And he who understands
No further word demands.

At Anchor

THE mast is bare, the sails are furled,
The water is as calm as love
That finds beyond the passionate world
A harbor that it dreamed not of.

The pines upon the shore reflect
The amber evening constellation,
There's nothing further to expect
But freedom from all expectation.

That is a joy not understood
By those who chase the wind; it seems
To hearts all flushed with hardihood
A dreary reckoning with dreams.

But I am one who rests content
When masts are bare and sails furled,
Knowing the way the wind went
After it blew me from the world.

Home Port

HAVE the boats all come home yet?
   Are the sails off the Sound?
From the masthead of sunset
   I look far around;
The blue water is empty now
Under Long Island's dark brow.

The day should never end at all,
   A happy day like this.
I must remember to recall
   When things go amiss
The fair wind that failed never
And how I wanted to live for ever.

Index of First Lines

A Note About the Author

ROBERT HILLYER is one of America's most distinguished and honored poets. He has received an impressive number of awards, including the Pulitzer Prize for Poetry in 1934. He is the author of many books of verse (the first was published when he was twenty-two), three novels, a book for the guidance of poets, *First Principles of Verse*, and a book for readers of poetry, *In Pursuit of Poetry*, as well as reviews, essays, short stories, and poems, which have been widely published.

Born in East Orange, New Jersey, on June 3, 1895, the poet is descended from General Gold Selleck Silliman of the Revolutionary War and is the grandson of General William Silliman Hillyer, one of General Grant's original staff. He was educated at Kent School in Connecticut, Harvard College, and the University of Copenhagen. A professor at Harvard for nineteen years, Robert Hillyer has taught also at Trinity College and Kenyon College, and is now H. Fletcher Brown Professor Emeritus of English Literature at the University of Delaware. He lives at present in Newark, Delaware.

Robert Hillyer is a member of the National Institute of Arts and Letters, a fellow of the American Academy of Arts and Sciences, a chancellor of the Academy of American Poets, and has twice served as president of the Poetry Society of America.

A Note on the Type

THE TEXT of this book was set on the Linotype in FAIR-
FIELD, a type face designed by the distinguished American artist and engraver, *Rudolph Ruzicka*. This type
displays the sober and sane qualities of a master craftsman
whose talent has long been dedicated to clarity. Rudolph
Ruzicka was born in Bohemia in 1883 and came to
America in 1894. He has designed and illustrated many
books and has created a considerable list of individual
prints in a variety of techniques.

Composed, printed, and bound by
KINGSPORT PRESS, INC., Kingsport, Tenn.
Paper manufactured by
S. D. WARREN CO., Boston.
Typography and binding design by
RUDOLPH RUZICKA

DATE DUE

PRINTED IN U.S.A.